A Place That's Known

A PLACE THAT'S KNOWN

Michael Pearson

University Press of Mississippi   *Jackson*

Designed by John A. Langston

The following publishers and individuals have generously given permission to use extended quotations from copyrighted works: From "Father and Son." Copyright © 1970 Cat Music Ltd. From James Seay, "It All Comes Together Outside the Restroom in Hogansville," from *Water Tables.* Copyright © 1974 Wesleyan University Press by permission of University Press of New England. From "Some Night Again," from *A Glass Face in the Rain,* Harper & Row, copyright © 1982 by William Stafford. From *The Poetry of Robert Frost,* edited by Edward Connery Lathem. Copyright © 1936 by Robert Frost. Copyright © 1964 by Lesley Frost Ballantine. Copyright © 1969 by Henry Holt and Company, Inc. Reprinted by permission of Henry Holt and Company, Inc. Published in the United Kingdom by Jonathan Cape. From William Carlos Williams. *Collected Poems: 1909–1939.* Vol I. Copyright © 1938 by New Directions Publishing Corporation. Reprinted by permission of New Directions. From *Selected Poems* by Langston Hughes. Copyright © 1924 by Alfred A. Knopf, Inc. and renewed 1952 by John Crowe Ransom. Reprinted by permission of the publisher. Lines from "Under Ben Bulben" are excerpted with permission of Macmillan Publishing Company from *The Poems of W. B. Yeats: A New Edition,* edited by Richard J. Finneran. Copyright © 1940 by Georgie Yeats, renewed 1968 by Bertha Georgie Yeats, Michael Butler Yeats, and Anne Yeats. Excerpt from "Casualty" from *Field Work* by Seamus Heaney. Copyright © 1976, 1979 by Seamus Heaney. Reprinted by permission of Farrar, Straus & Giroux, Inc., and Faber and Faber Limited.

CIP data appear on page 258.

For Shane, Ian and Owen

I have been after an adventure all my life, a pure dispassionate adventure, such as befell early and heroic voyagers.

—Robert Louis Stevenson,
Travels With a Donkey

History is as light as individual life, unbearably light, light as a feather, as dust swirling into the air, as whatever will no longer exist tomorrow.
—Milan Kundera,
The Unbearable Lightness of Being

. . . and find a place that's known to God alone . . .

—J. Keirn Brennan
and Ernest R. Ball,
"Let the Rest of the World Go By"

Contents

Prologue

The essays in this book are concerned with how memory and imagination affect our feelings about place, how fathers and sons align themselves in the world, how literature re-presents experience. These narratives, reminiscences and reportage, are all nonfiction, but many use the techniques of fiction, for finally the book seeks a truth of the heart, embedded in people and place and the imagination. However, I have always sought historical accuracy, and only in the Georgia chapter have some of the situations and the characters' names been changed to protect certain individuals' privacy.

This is also a book *about* stories, the sort one can find in literature, in life, in dreams. And perhaps the book is ultimately concerned with how such threads of light come together to form our vision of the world and our place in it, how such stories help us to see as we grope along in the dark.

As a child I read hoping to learn everything, so I could be like my father.

> —Annie Dillard,
> *An American Childhood*

As a child I read hoping to find a father, a voice that was wise, funny, strong, hopeful. I discovered it at times in books, rarely in the world around me. I heard that voice, full of compassion and truth, in the tones of Pip and David Copperfield, in Huck Finn and Holden Caulfield, in Nick Carraway and Jack Burden. Later, when I was old enough to reach a wider world, I heard it coming from the stories of Zora Neale Hurston, Flaubert, Walker Percy, Hawthorne. I heard it in *Tom Jones* and *Don Quixote*. Now I hear such understanding in Toni Morrison, Anne Tyler, Lee Smith, Cormac McCarthy, Josephine Humphreys, and others. Eudora Welty once said, "It is to me the voice of the story or the poem itself. The cadence, whatever it is that asks you to believe, the feeling that resides in the printed word, reaches me through the reader-voice." The desire to listen, as Welty suggests, is intricately connected to the compulsion to write, the need to make or record stories.

The voices that I heard in stories made me wonder about the voice behind each story. As a boy I tried to imagine the writers who created the tales. Who were these people who lived behind the words and, for me, in them? Homer, Shakespeare, Chaucer, Emily Brontë,

Edith Wharton, Jack London. How had they learned enough and lived enough to write so perceptively? I imagined that they had lived close to a fiery romantic truth, as I supposed my own father had. My grandfather, blind before my father was born, was a man whose eyes were blank mirrors of my father's face. I reasoned that a father who could never see his son might always judge him too harshly or not honestly enough. However, a father who was blind, I assumed, would force a son to look more carefully at everything in the world, for the father's sake and his own. My own father had fought in the South Pacific in World War II. He had been brave, but for modesty's sake, I believed, he hardly ever spoke about the war. Nevertheless, the pictures from his battalion's album told a gruesome, exuberant story: the charred, twisted remains of a Japanese sniper, his scream frozen onto his face by an American flame thrower; or a group of young half-naked Seabees, dressed in grass skirts and gathered in a careless line, smiling like the Rockettes at Radio City Music Hall. My father had lived. These pictures told me so.

But somewhere along the way, disappointments had blurred the smiling images in the photographs. My father's face occasionally lighted playfully in a way that reminded me of those spirited looks from Tarawa and Okinawa. In those pictures his face, squinting in the burning sun, was often flushed with expectation, it seemed to me, eager to encounter the world, despite the tragedy around him. I never knew what gradually smothered much of the warmth and joy in his life. Responsibilities? The wrong job? Dreams left unrealized? But I was certain that I wanted to find a way of living that demanded that I *live* and make sense of that life. I had the same fear that Annie Dillard expressed in *An American Childhood*, that "I would wake on my deathbed and say, What was that?" Therefore, very early on, observing some of the disappointment and despair that crackled in the air around me like nuclear fallout, I decided to find a vocation, and a *calling* implied some voices leading the way. In stories I heard these voices. The books I read were often filled with sadness, but their source always seemed to be knowledge and the joy that comes from it. I came to the conclusion that writers live fully because they are pilgrims, not merely tourists. To be writers they had to be observant, watching for signs, for meaning. Such attentiveness, I felt, would bring the world to life.

I was fourteen years old when I found a used paperback copy of Herman Wouk's *Youngblood Hawke* in a bookstore on Fordham Road in the Bronx. It was Christmas vacation, but what I remember of that time has little to do with presents or holiday cheer. Instead, I remember reading about Youngblood Hawke, an untutored genius, a natural writer. I read his story in my bedroom until my eyes ached and burned, until the very air seemed to turn white. The book, 878 pages long, kept me in my room, except for food and drink, brief conversations, and other necessities, for days. It was the story that I needed at the time.

Up to that point, my life had been encompassed by nuns and priests, by baptisms and confirmations and confessions, by the safe harbor of neighbors and schoolmates and the known—Al's Delicatessen, Sarah's Candy Store, St. Philip Neri Church, Harris Field. Anger and depression were just beginning to appear around me like deformed faces in a lifting fog. The more alcohol or indecipherable rage intruded on my life the more I turned inward, looking for a path away through the imagination. But rather than running from pain, perhaps I was looking for an explanation of it, exploring adventurously inside. As Eudora Welty has said, "A sheltered life can be a daring life as well. For all serious daring starts within."

Like many adolescents I dreamt of glory on the football field or basketball court. But I was small and smart enough to know the chances against becoming Johnny Unitas or Bob Cousy. When I rearranged the shape of furious loneness that my fourteen-year-old life often took and became Youngblood Hawke for hour after hour, day after day, during that Christmas vacation, at first I saw only the Romantic possibilities. The novel fit the curve of my adolescent yearnings like a complementary puzzle piece. From Hovey, Kentucky, Hawke was, like me, a small-town boy (198th St. and the Grand Concourse was like a small town, an insular world), and he became an overnight success. Like my father, Hawke had been a Seabee, but unlike him Hawke had fought unwaveringly to bring his dreams to life. *Youngblood Hawke* was the Horatio Alger story, the perfect adolescent myth, retold by Herman Wouk as the story of the rocket-like rise of an unkempt, gargantuan innocent who became a Pulitzer Prize winner. The picture on my Signet paperback cover, frayed and water-stained, of a shapely older woman, naked and in the embrace of a square-jawed young novelist, increased the attractiveness of the book for me.

Youngblood Hawke dramatized the idea that the world can change remarkably in a short period of time. Between 1946 and 1953 Youngblood Hawke wrote five books, each deeper than the one before it. For the first book he received a check for five thousand dollars, more money than I could imagine at that time ever saving. By the end of the novel, like a character in a tale from the *Arabian Nights*, Hawke was a millionaire. Wouk said that Hawke "wielded his gifts like a conquistador to re-enact the American dream." From the outset, Hawke knew what he wanted. And he had confidence. When his first editor admonished him for being too optimistic about his chances as a writer, saying, "Well, it's a dream that most people have and few reach," Hawke replied simply, "I'll reach it."

In Hawke's voice I learned the first lesson that I needed to hear: "I'll reach it." In the context of reading his story, I saw my previous heroes, New York Giants football players Jimmy Patton and Sam Huff, fade and literary names come into sharper focus—Dickens, Twain, Mann, Proust.

After that Christmas vacation, as I sat dreaming at my desk at Mount St. Michael High School, I saw myself in Hawke, who had been "a boy of intense if intermittent religiosity." Going to Catholic school in those days meant intense religiosity; the flesh made spiritual commitments intermittent, though. Hawke had three women in his life. He fell into a wild affair with Frieda Winter, a sophisticated older woman. (At fourteen, to me all women seemed older and sophisticated). Hawke's true love in the story, however, was Jeanne Green. She was steady, beautiful, ironic, the woman every fourteen-year-old boy wants to marry, expects to marry. The third woman in his life was his mother; his father was absent. I felt as if I understood that part of the story well. Like Dostoevsky, Hawke was an epileptic. Even the big, strong mountain boy had his hidden weaknesses, like the rest of us.

In a certain way, even at fourteen years old, I realized that *Youngblood Hawke* was a tale of adolescence. Hawke's life was pulsing with experience. In a few short years he lived many lives. His life seemed like my adolescence, like all adolescence. There was a clear warning in the story: exorbitance, finally, brings disaster. A combination of extravagance and innocence eventually levelled him, but even brought to earth Hawke seemed to me a magnificent jumble of pride and stammering modesty, awkwardness and rough power. He died, but he left behind something of value, his books.

Arthur Hawke knew Hovey, Kentucky, "as a prisoner knows his cell." That's how I knew the Bronx. Hawke escaped through writing. I knew at fourteen that I would, too. I knew also that, like him, I had fallen in love with words and the call of stories. Living, for me, would always be part of listening to and retelling stories. The voices I heard in stories, whispering like adoptive fathers, told me to watch and wait, told me that living and imagining are one and the same, told me that story-telling is not merely a stay against despair but an act of faith, a way of living, of being alive.

When I reread *Youngblood Hawke* recently, I knew right away that it wasn't the book I had thought it to be over twenty-five years ago. As one critic said of Wouk, "Sometimes he plods so doggedly that you begin to admire him more for his stamina than his storytelling." Now the story seems to me contrived and overblown. If written today, it would be a ripe plum to be plucked by some producer for a television mini-series, drifting as the novel does from court case to McCarthy hearings, from publishing boardrooms to elegant bedrooms. But as I read it through again a quarter of a century later, I found myself enjoying parts of it. More than anything, though, it was something of a ghost reading: I was remembering myself back then as I fell headlong into that story. I don't regret remembering the book with such pleasure over the years or realizing with certainty what

I suspected for a long time—that the novel definitely is not great literature. It's not always great literature that opens the door to the wider world for us. Sometimes it's a silly half-success that makes us pick up our heads and listen, and listening we may hear other voices, far more beautiful and lasting, in books and the world about us.

THE PAST

So we beat on, boats against the current, borne back ceaselessly into the past.
> —F. Scott Fitzgerald,
> *The Great Gatsby*

Life is history, full of stories.
> —Gretel Ehrlich,
> *Islands, the Universe, Home*

CHAPTER I

THE BRONX / MAINE

The Bronx, no thonx

—Ogden Nash

Two hours before Brother Placid smiled beatifically at us in our seventh grade geography class, his eyes magnified into hypnotic orbs by glasses thicker than the concrete walls of a bomb shelter, we had all been frozen into a terrible silence by Brother Boniface, our French teacher. There were forty-six of us in the boys' seventh grade class, but only the forty-two elite took French. I'm not sure what the disgraced four did—suffer through remedial math, say the rosary, or work in the bowels of the school with the janitor. But anything would have been better than French with Brother Boniface.

Boniface had slick dark hair and was tall, pale, and soft looking. He had a doughy complexion and was rounded at all the edges but had none of the jollity we often ascribe to chubby people. He spoke with a sneering lisp, an inflection that rose up like a sharpened dagger. In his class I learned little French, but I developed the art of watchfulness. Brother Boniface was a master of sarcasm. He seemed to be able to see into our souls, find where we were most vulnerable, and use words like a thumb against a pressure point.

"What does the word '*illettré*' mean, Mr. Slater?"

Silence.

"What's the problem, Mr. Slater, too much time jumping rope with the girls and not enough doing your homework?"

A more dangerous silence. Blood exploded into Slater's face, fueled by both shame and anger. We all sat there thinking: here's Brother Boniface, the most effeminate of all our teachers, certainly more so than any of the nuns we knew, an Oscar Wilde with all the venom but none of the wit, challenging someone else's sexuality. We all sat there hoping: don't look at me; stick with Slater. Torture him if you must until the bell rings. In the name of the Father, the Son, and the Holy Ghost, Amen.

On this day Boniface pranced in front of us, his eyebrows raised in a permanent dare, his tongue making literal the metaphor of the lash. But somehow Gerald "Gump" O'Mannly had momentarily slipped back into a state of antediluvian innocence in the last seat in the third row: he had for a minute forgotten the danger, and by the time the dam broke it was too late to repair the damage. Out of the corner of my eye I saw him smile, heard him giggle, caught the white flash of an exchanged note. Gump realized his personal catastrophe a split second after I did. All of a sudden he seemed to be alone in midair like a cartoon character who sees the chasm only after he has run far off the edge of the cliff.

Brother Boniface stood over him.

"Mr. O'Mannly?" His voice was like an oiled machine. "A love note, perhaps?" The faces of the forty-two boys in the room twisted into sickly smiles. The class pulse sped up, mouths went dry, armpits moistened. Then there was that awful collective thrill, the smell of blood. Like all good Catholics we prayed fervently for the martyr, hoping the beast would be appeased before he eyed us.

Boniface turned his back and walked to the front of the room, his robes swishing against the desks, his crucifix bobbing at his side. He faced us and smiled. Acid ran through our intestines.

"Mr. O'Mannly, come up here please." He said it sweetly, as if it were possible that he planned to forget the whole matter and forgive the transgression. But the silence was as thick as a dust cloud, making our breathing shallow in anticipation of what we knew would happen. Gump knew, too. As he shuffled up the aisle, he reminded me of Boniface, soft and doughy, but somehow I already saw Gump's curly brown hair and open Irish face framed in a gallery of martyrs.

"Bend over, Mr. O'Mannly," he said in the kind of gently encouraging tone one might expect to hear an

The Bronx/Maine

Oxford-educated Japanese interrogator use on a downed British pilot in an old war film.

O'Mannly bent over the front desk and looked briefly at the forty-one faces fastened on his shrinking smile. Brother Boniface went to the closet as slowly as someone performing a repetition in a respected ceremony, a baptism or confirmation. Reaching into the shadows he pulled out a wooden paddle, eighteen inches long, six inches wide, and two inches thick. It had the useful, polished look of an instrument carved out of oak.

Boniface planted himself behind Gump, a little to the side, spreading his feet wide, like a cleanup hitter on a baseball team. He moved the fingers of his left hand along the paddle, caressing for a moment the perfect smoothness of the wood, and then his right hand shot out like a viper's tongue from the black folds of his clerical robes. He grabbed the paddle and raised it high, lifting it away from his body. Down it came, swiftly and with a loud "thwack," making a sound that, in apparent defiance of the laws of physics, cracked the silence before the wood ever touched Gump. All of us jerked back at the same instant, pulled by the same string of sympathy and fear. It happened again. And once again.

By the fourth time Brother Boniface raised his arm, tears had welled up in Gump's eyes. Along with everyone else, I looked intently into the grain of my desk as if the answer to some unstated question lay hidden there. Each time Boniface raised his hand, he took longer to let it descend. This time he stopped.

"Mr. O'Mannly, get some paper towels from the bathroom and clean that up!" As Gump left the room, the lunch bell rang, and it was only as I got to the front of the class on my way out the door that I saw the curling pool of urine by the front desk and realized what had happened. I never said anything to Gerald about it. I don't know if anyone ever did.

We spent recess in the playground behind the school. The girls lined up on one side, the boys on the other, as if we were practicing for future dances, clinging desperately to our groups and eyeing each other suspiciously.

In the fifth grade, girls and boys had been separated into different classes, in different sections of the school, the theory being, I assumed, that only the twelve-inch-thick cinder block walls could stop us from consummating a volcanic prepubescent lust. As for me, the nuns should not have feared—it was football and basketball I dreamed of, of sailing ships and mountain climbing. The distant aching we had begun to feel for girls would not for a few years become a throbbing desire. But in the final analysis, the nuns may have been right, for by the time most of us reached high school we were sex-crazed imbeciles, drooling, mumbling, and walking into walls when a girl appeared. This all happened, ironically, at about the same time the girls I knew began to model their behavior on the lives of the saints.

But in the seventh grade the boys stuck together to play hunter or johnny-on-the-pony or punchball. St. Philip Neri stood on the edge of Villa Avenue, a five-block section as thick with Italians as Sicily. On Villa Avenue they seemed to swallow their syllables along with their tomato sauce: Anthony was always "Antony." But Christian names were rarely used anyway; instead there were nicknames: Miser or Little Man or BigAss. These names always alluded to some personality trait or physical characteristic. Miser was notoriously cheap, Little Man had a moustache at eight years old, and BigAss . . . well, these were not subtle namings.

For most games it was the Irish against the Italians, which meant those with last names beginning with O on one side and those with names ending in O on the other. We played intensely, untucking our white shirts and twisting our maroon ties. Streaks of perspiration dried into rivulets on our cheeks. Our shoes were scuffed, our hands dirty. By the time we returned to the classroom we had nearly forgotten Brother Boniface and Gerald O'Mannly.

Brother Placid had been our geography teacher for three weeks, replacing someone on leave. It had taken fifteen school days for most of us to figure out that he was the genuine article, as calm and myopic as he appeared to be. He was short and his glasses gave a distant, unfocused look to his entire face. He seemed to be submerged in water. As I think back on it he may have been as saintly as Singer's Gimpel the Fool, but at the time we saw him as an answer to our prayers—a brother who could be duped by our skillful wiles and tricks. Of course, with the wisdom of retrospect, I realize he must have been a saint, for our tricks had little subtlety. Nevertheless, he was a release valve, allowing some of the pressure built by our other teachers to hiss away.

On this day we pulled our two most masterful rebellions. His class was inconceivably boring. Even as I think about it now it's hard to recapture the matchless level of dullness he almost always achieved. He could take the most dramatic subject and make it mundane; a trip through ancient Egypt became as drab as a ride on a local bus. Or he could take the simplest subject and complicate it beyond belief. We spent a full two weeks listening to him lecture about how milk arrived in the food stores. He required us to take meticulous notes about cows and forty-gallon milk cans and trucks and highways, until the very thought of milk made us nauseous. Most of us depended upon Billy Brown or Frankie Bartoletti to take notes. The rest of us spent the time more usefully—daydreaming or checking wind currents before we fired another round of spitballs.

When Brother Placid came into the classroom that afternoon, his face was a blur and his voice was soft and remote. Immediately he began reviewing the process by which milk finds its way from farms to food stores. "Forty-gallon cans . . . loaded onto trucks . . . highways to the city . . ." his voice droned on as he turned his back on us and wrote notes on the board.

That's when the movement started. As far as I could

The Bronx/Maine

tell no one person moved first. Rather, everyone seemed to move at the same time, as if some group instinct were at work. Forty-six desks softly squeaked forward. Brother Placid continued to speak, a hum reverberating off the chalkboard. The desks continued to move. When he turned around to face us, his eyes widened and popped for a moment into clear focus. His head snapped back. All forty-six desks were squeezed up to the front of the room, within inches of him. In the back of the room was a space large enough to hold a dance. He never said anything. At the time I was certain we had surprised him into catatonia. Now my guess is that he saw himself as a medieval monk. We were his hair shirt. He turned back to the board and continued his notes. The beast with forty-six heads once again began to move. The next time Brother Placid turned around he nearly fell forward into the gaping space in front of him. All the desks were crammed into the rear, hugging the far wall. Twenty feet of space separated us from him, and for a second he appeared to totter on the brink of crumbling into the emptiness.

His lesson went on, but encouraged by our achievements we dared greater things. Jimmy Buffano led the way. He slid from his desk and slithered across the room, quietly entering the coat closets. Then Timothy O'Leary. Then Joseph Pagliari. Then another and another, until a full one-third of the class was laughing and elbowing each other in the darkness, listening to perts—by advertisers, clothing designers, architects—travel has become today an even more necessary escape. And Camus's remark seems even more true: "Travel brings us back to ourselves." Travel cuts us off from our typical moorings, separates us from familiar surroundings, from the things that define us but confine us as well. As the historian Eric Leed says, "Among strangers a new sense of selfhood can be tried on like a costume." In a sense, travel is a search for immortality, a race against the sun.

My first trips were in a black-and-white 1951 Ford with a stick shift on the column and the inescapable smell of perfume and cigarette smoke in the upholstery. Each summer for two weeks in July or August my father would shed his job as a construction worker like some repulsive dead skin and take my mother, my sister, and me to Maine. He was used to rising early and would be outside our apartment shortly after sunrise, checking the oil and buffing the chrome. By the time we got up and packed the car it was midmorning.

The road swirled by in a montage of games and rituals. My sister and I sat in the back seat layered in turkey sandwiches, bottles of root beer, bags of potato chips, coloring books, puzzles, teddy bears, and dolls. As the years went by the layers changed to movie magazines and baseball cards or paperbacks and nail polish. We named the capitals or searched for license plates. All went well unless my father lost his way, for he would

the even more distant strains of Brother Placid's voice, "Milk cans . . . milk . . . pasteurized. . . ."

A light struck us like God's voice. It streamed in through the door that had been opened by Brother Bruce, the principal. He was obviously more worldly than Brother Placid, and when he came into the room on a routine visit decided he wanted a logical explanation for so many missing faces. I think the theory of original sin led him to the closets.

That afternoon after school we waited outside Brother Bruce's room to receive our shots. We took them, one at a time, in privacy, for Brother Bruce had none of the smiling sadism of Brother Boniface. The shots stung anyway, but the stinging faded quickly. In another year and a few months I would be in high school, which I knew meant more of the same. Things would be even stricter: Brother Charles Daniels, the Dean of Discipline, would turn out to be the most rigorously and consistently unsmiling man I was to know before or since; the concept of detention would be raised to new heights, the Marist Brothers knowing as much about torture as the North Koreans in the early fifties; and ordinary regimentation and rules—haircuts and shoeshines and bookbags—would become as sacred as the Ten Commandments.

New York City led me toward Maine. For me much of the Bronx was corridors and alleyways, rules and restrictions, a maze of "don'ts" and punishments, of stair-wells and subway tunnels. The squat five- and six-story apartment houses rose up, and although they didn't block the sun, they contrived with the ever-present soot-covered clouds to splinter the sun's rays into slivers of light lost in the gray angles of the buildings.

By midsummer of each year, after eleven months in the Bronx, the very air seemed stale, the buildings hollow, the rattle from the Independent subway line in front of my bedroom window ominous. The idea of spending two weeks in Maine stirred up dreams of clear lakes glistening in the still morning and pine needles spinning lazily in the afternoon breeze. Like Henry Adams, for me the city was restraint and law. But the country was "liberty, diversity, outlawry, the endless delight of mere sense impression given by nature for nothing, and breathed by boys without knowing it." In the summer of 1962 the Bronx was my geographic home, but Maine was my spiritual one.

When the world vanishes, I will come back here
by the power of my dreams and create it again,
starting where that clear depth in the mountain
lake began, where you swam one night across the
moonlight and I thought: Still, it's good, though
it has to end.

—William Stafford,
"Some Night Again"

THE PAST

The road is better than the inn.

—Cervantes

I've always felt at home on the road. In motion, I'm contemplative. I understand what Kerouac meant b[...] purity of the road, where motion connects travel[...] the world but also allows them some distance fro[...] The black blur of the highway, the rippling curv[...] country routes, the narrow side streets of the cit[...] bring the world into focus for me. On a blistering [...] gust afternoon I can glimpse my own reflection in t[...] mirages of heat and tar that tease us forward. In t[...] black pools, disappearing like thoughts in a drea[...] find myself.

The need to escape the familiar is as universal as [...] stories of Odysseus and Huck Finn, the need for [...] discovery as old as humankind. Like Robinson Cru[...] we are castaways looking for footprints on the sh[...] We are all wayfarers longing for a wilderness of new [...] unexpected experiences in which to find our freed[...] especially today when best-selling psychology bo[...] tell us who we are and Hollywood tells us who [...] should want to be, when the only wilderness left to [...] plore is the one we discover through the force of [...] imaginations.

Travel was once for philosophers. Now it's for tou[...] ists. Snapshots have replaced ideas. Wanderers ha[...] been shoved from the path by tour guides. But perha[...] because experience has been packaged for us by the e[...]

The Bronx/Maine

never ask directions but would drive along in a sullen rage that occasionally erupted into mumbled curses.

But from the moment I sat down in the back seat of the car, the trip seemed like a necessary departure. I was on the road, a nomad, and my blood received signals from ancestors a thousand years before. This was the original human condition, to travel. Even my father was transformed. Leaving the job he hated behind him, he turned into a kindly stranger. The journey made us believe in such transformations. Even when my sister and I got older and the transformations were far less dramatic and our capacity to accept such illusions diminished, we believed these transient changes were part of passage from the city.

We drove along vaguely remembered roads and turnpikes, stopped at strangely familiar picnic areas, and watched the dusk drop slowly like a dark translucent curtain. Then we would sing for the last hour of the ride—the Seabee's theme, the Marine Hymn, Christmas songs, and a medley of George M. Cohan tunes. But we always ended with my father, in a soft tenor voice I remember hearing only on those trips to Maine, singing "Let the Rest of the World Go By":

> With someone like you
> a pal so good and true
> I'd like to leave it all behind
> and go and find

a place that's known
to God alone,
just a spot to call our own.
We'll find perfect peace
where joys will never cease,
somewhere beneath the starry skies.
We'll build a sweet little nest,
somewhere in the West,
and let the rest of the world go by.

Our voices rose up with his, and in the car we were a chorus, a family. We moved along, in the world but somehow not of it, for we were in motion, all changing and new. Everything was left behind—school, my father's rotten jobs, the unsympathetic foremen, careless co-workers, the heat, the tiny apartment that bred my father's sour looks and angry words—as we sang, "We'll find perfect peace . . . joys will never cease." And we believed it.

I believed in Maine. Maine was my Mississippi River, my green light on a distant dock, my Walden Pond. It was my escape from the stolid, faded-brick atmosphere of the Bronx. It was my belief in days filled with something other than nuns and brothers, religion bees, Stations of the Cross, and silent obedience, other than my father's angry silences, the treeless streets, and the dreary subway platforms. I turned twelve the last summer I went to Maine, in 1962. The next fall Khrushchev and Kennedy would convince me of my own mortality, of the impossibility of finding a safe haven, but in the spring of my seventh grade year I still believed in escape.

In Maine my dreams began. Each summer I would see the same children, play the same games, and reimagine my life. In the mornings we hunted for blueberries, filling old coffee cans until we heard our names called for breakfast. In the afternoons we swam or played horseshoes or hugged the shoreline in canoes. In the evening, after dinner, we waged pine cone wars, storing hundreds of grenade-like cones and waiting breathlessly in the forests for our enemies. Each day lasted an eternity. Everything had a magic to it.

My first memory is of Maine. I was four years old, and my parents had told me not to go near the boathouse. But the boathouse, with its dark green doors, stood streaked in the shadows of tall pines, only a hundred feet from our cabin. What four-year-old could resist such a temptation? When I swung the creaking boathouse door open and squinted through the cobwebs that laced the entranceway, I saw the rectangle of water shimmering like jade in moonlight. The perimeter of the boathouse, a walkway about three feet wide, was gritty with sand. The only sounds were the distant riffling of pine needles in the breeze and the lake lapping like hushed speech against the inner walls.

It's the murmur of the lake I remember hearing as I stumbled and fell, as slowly and cinematically as in a dream, into the water. I didn't know how to swim and the water was over my head. I vividly recall walking under water until I reached the dock just outside the boathouse and climbed up the shaky wooden ladder. Four-year-olds most likely don't walk under water, but that is my memory, and it's probably healthier than a recollection that I walked on top of it.

I rose up, shaking the water from me like sparks into the gathering darkness, to stand face-to-face with an old man who lived down the road. He never asked me what happened, just smiled as if it were normal for a young boy to rise from the water fully clothed, as evening began. He patted my head like a preacher in a country baptism. I snuck back into the cabin, went upstairs, changed my clothes, and lay dreaming on the bed. Reaching my arm up to feel the rough grain of one of the rafters, I breathed in the wood, the musty heat, and the smell of my own immortality.

Nearly a decade later, at twelve, I still believed in Maine and in my own invincibility. In Maine anything was possible. Brothers and nuns were in another world, another time. I could be Kit Carson or a Viking or Jimmy Patton, whose New York Giants football card I carried with me as I carried the memory of *The Vikings*, the only movie my father ever took me to see. In Maine my father became for me a man made of dreams and memories. There was no Durella's Bar for him to stop in on his way home from his construction job. In our small apartment in the Bronx the exit door opened into the living room, and if my father was not home before dinner time, we knew what to expect. My sister and I would sit on the sofa, huddled next to my mother, protecting her and protected by her, until the key clicked in the door and a hot bolt of fear shot through my stomach as the door banged open and he staggered in, his eyes angry slits. The room squeezed in on us, and we built a wall against his slurred insults.

The lake was an open world. There were no corridors or alleyways as there were in the Bronx. In the morning the sun melted onto the water, making diamonds of light along the surface. When storms arose, they didn't sneak around corners but tumbled in, first announcing themselves in the distance. Mail arrived every morning at eleven o'clock on the mail boat, the tourists smiling awkwardly as the mate handed one of us a packet of letters. Lunch was always at noon, and in the early afternoon we generally walked into town, taking the shortcut, a path behind the cabin that led past Goldthwaite's Antiques to Irving's Grocery, which sold everything from Charleston Chews to bloodworms. Each day was a comforting ritual. The world seemed fixed and permanent, like the lake itself.

Long Lake stretched out as wide and as far as a boy's dreams. About a mile and a half to the north stood an island, and the ten miles of lake beyond it seemed as mysterious and exotic to me as Tibet. The lake, which snakes thirteen miles from Naples to Harrison, is about two miles at its widest. It narrows as it flows into

Brandy Pond in the south and eventually connects through the Songo River, like a twisting umbilical cord, to the twenty-mile-wide Sebago Lake. I knew every inch of my corner of Long Lake. I paddled the coves, roamed along the shore, and dreamed my way through the piney woods. I understood how Nathaniel Hawthorne felt when he told a friend, "I lived in Maine like a bird of the air, so perfect was the freedom I enjoyed."

On bright, clear mornings the water stood like beveled glass, showing the sandy bottom out beyond the end of the dock. On stormy afternoons, with dark clouds frowning in the northeast, whitecaps snapped and foamed across the lake. At times the wind would gust even on a cloudless day and spread itself like a flapping sheet across the water. When I was twelve I swam across the lake. It took me a little over an hour, and when I rose on the other side I was dizzy with fatigue and a sense of my own glory. The next day in the newspaper there was a picture of Fred Baldasare, the scuba diver from California who had swum the English Channel underwater. At the time I felt cheated that my photograph was not alongside his.

That night I counted twelve shooting stars, one for each year I had lived. I lay on the dock dreaming of bearded Vikings and Kit Carson and Jimmy Patton, of my own exploring, my fame and success. At twelve, I had spent most of my life dreaming. I walked through the cemetery at the top of the road, expecting ghosts and black-cloaked figures to appear. I sat under heavy oaks thinking of Tippy, the sad-eyed dog who be-friended me every summer until one July it simply was no longer there. I imagined a world as open and clear as the lake—away from the confines of the classroom and our one-bedroom apartment in the Bronx, where I hid in books and reveries from the words of Brother Boni-face or the glassy-eyed stare of my father.

In Maine dreams of escape seemed substantial, as real as the lake itself. Then one day two girls appeared, and after that all I dreamt of was them. One was sixteen, a waitress in town who boarded at the lodge adjacent to our cabin. She was as thin as Olive Oyl and had the same stringy brown hair, but to me she was unimagin-ably old and experienced, a Marilyn Monroe without the blonde hair, the cleavage, the beautiful face. The other girl was my age and pretty enough to make my heart jump whenever she looked in my direction. The sixteen-year-old brought me up to her room one day, and with the Shirelles singing "Soldier Boy" on the ra-dio, she put her tongue in my mouth and my hands on her tiny breasts, changing my dreams immediately. Later that summer when I saw *Splendor in the Grass* at the drive-in I felt I understood it, and also perhaps why Marilyn Monroe took all those pills: each had something to do with unrequited love. The sloe-eyed younger girl, who had the same blonde hair and cooing voice as Marilyn, flirted with me but never let me know outside of hinting what worlds lay beyond frontier ad-venture and football.

The Bronx/Maine

I grew up and never returned to Maine with my family. My father sold his car ("a headache in the city") and drank more (the construction trade wasn't the same) and worked less. By that fall, America was already becoming too entangled in the jungles of Vietnam to extricate itself easily. There were race riots at Ole Miss that made us contemplate our lily-white lives. And the Cuban missile crisis sent most of us in St. Philip Neri parish to church or to our rosary beads. I was pretty sure the world was going to explode, and when it didn't it seemed to me so different that it might as well have.

As I was going home on Labor Day weekend in 1962, the car radio announced that e. e. cummings had died in North Conway, New Hampshire, and even though I hardly knew his name then and would not for years read John Logan's poem about his death, I already sensed that "death is not a problem to be solved but a mystery to be entered into." As we drove past Woodlawn Cemetery and headed toward the Grand Concourse and our apartment in the Bronx, Gene Chandler boasted in bass tones on the radio, "Nothing can stop me now . . . I'm the Duke of Earl." In the years after that summer of 1962 in Maine, I was never again quite so sure about the world as Chandler seemed to be.

In a quarter of a century the picture of the world can change many times over. Vietnam, Woodstock, Watergate, Martin Luther King—the images broke against the sky like those shooting stars I had seen. But my memories of Maine stayed the same, and although I feared going back and finding that the place had changed horribly, like an old friend crippled with disease, I longed to see it once again, to see if Eric Leed's prediction were true that "man's return to paradise invariably brings its destruction. . . ."

Every man has to stand in front of the house of his childhood in order to recover himself.
—Soren Kierkegaard

Don't look behind. Something may be gaining on you.

—Satchel Paige

Roger Kahn once said that to age with dignity and with courage cuts close to what it is to be a man. As I drive down Route 302 in Maine toward Naples with my mother and two of my sons in the car with me, I can't help thinking about how I've aged and wondering if the town and the lake and the past they hold in them will tell me something I don't know.

My mother, who will be eighty in a few months, seems not to have changed in the thirty years that have passed since we traveled this road when I was a child. The world surprises her, takes her off guard, the same way it did then. She is ready, with my sons, to shoot a foul shot, throw a Frisbee, or wield a golf club at the driving range. She does all this with a girlish awkwardness but a boyish intensity. On the road she has no sense of direction and depends upon the kindness of fate to direct her, but she has a strength that comes from optimism, the same strength she always shared on the sofa in that cramped apartment in the Bronx.

My sons Ian, who is fourteen, and Owen, who is nine, play twenty-one questions as we drive along. Watching my mother and them, I see my own life repeated. I feel as E. B. White did when he wrote in "Once More to the Lake" of living a dual existence, being both father and son, experiencing both past and present. The boys are very different, but in them I see parts of myself, my loves, my flaws. For the most part they have taken the best and discarded the rest, but I look at them and see myself at nine and fourteen, whipsaw thin, bright-eyed, hungry for the future.

We drive along 302 through Bridgton, which seems less dour than I remember it, and pass the old Catholic church we used to attend on summer Sundays. Its facade is the same, but it's now a clothing store, stained-glass windows replaced with clear glass and smartly dressed mannequins. This is a bad omen, but Bridgton actually is handsomer than my memory of it, and the country road leading toward Naples is uncluttered and apparently unchanged. In Naples we turn left at the town cemetery, drive past the graves we walked by as children, skittish in those summer nights filled with the voices of ghosts, and bounce along the rutted drive that leads down to the lake and the cabin from twenty-five years ago.

At first glance, things have changed. The boathouse is gone—lost, we're told, in a lightning storm. The lodge, which had once stood on the rocky shoreline, burnt down. The new owner, from a suburb of New York City, lives in a modern house on the hill, and in some sad imitation of Levittown put a chainlink fence up to separate his property from his neighbors.

The cabin I knew every inch of still stands, but precariously, it seems. The bright yellow I remember is now an ash gray that at first looks to be the result of a fire. But it's neglect, not flames, that has left its mark—broken windows, peeling paint, torn screens, a sagging roof.

I stand on the edge of the dock and look down at the sandy bottom of the lake. Some things have not changed: the lake is as pure as memory, clear and still. Then I hear a voice and look up to see a man on the porch of the old King place next door. It's been more than twenty-five years since I've seen him, but without hesitation I call out, "Billy—Billy King!" as if I were twelve again and had seen him the night before. Somehow he recognizes me, despite the years, the inches, the moustache. Except for his gray hair, he looks exactly as he did at eighteen, although I don't recall his runner's thinness. His eyes reflect the same innocent light. He still holds himself boyishly, ready, it appears, to fly off. His family used to call him "Bird"—perhaps they sensed the same inclination to flight.

For fifteen minutes he tells us all he can about the changes in real estate, the summer crowd, the town. But he seems to rush past those stories, anxious to tell another.

"I guess you're wondering why my hair is so short," he says. My mother and I just look at him and nod noncommittally. To say "yes" would be to acknowledge that we thought his hair too short. I thought it looked the same length it had been when he was twenty, the last time I had seen him. To say "no" would be to suggest we weren't paying attention or didn't care. So we both nodded ambiguously, saying "yes," "no," and "maybe" all at the same time.

"I've just finished chemotherapy. Last December I was diagnosed with a lymphoma . . ."

As he describes his illness, I realize how frail his legs are, as thin as a sparrow's.

"You look good. Thank God you're feeling better," my mother and I say in unison. And the simple, astounding fact is that he does look good, the same—as if he were twenty and were about to walk from his house to our cabin in the gathering dusk to play canasta and laugh until long after night had fallen, the moths had wearied themselves against the window screen, and the crickets' song had disappeared into itself.

As we talk about the dying past, my sons toss a football near the cabin. I listen to Billy but glance at them, caught between the past and the future, feeling like a traveller in time. The present seems as slippery as tomorrow and as difficult to grasp as yesterday. The ball hangs at the top of its arc, its stitches smiling a cartoon moonface. And time, for a moment, stands still.

> *Standing on the shore, I once more cast my line*
> *into the stream and found the dream to be real*
> *and the fable true.*
>
> —Henry David Thoreau

Our cabin is on Brandy Pond, named, legend has it, because a case of brandy fell off one of the canal boats in the mid-1800s and disappeared into its depths. I rented a place in Fox Hollow Cabins on Brandy Pond sight unseen because the names felt right. Now, as we turn off Songo Locks Road onto Pine Rock Road, twisting our way a few miles back into the woods, I sense my intuition was good. The cabin sits a few feet from the water's edge, a gently curving bay made into a perfect crescent by the stone retaining wall built along the shore. The sun unrolls in a purple ribbon of light in the distance, sending threads of dark orange onto the water.

Ian, Owen, and I swim in the lake. It is purer than I imagined it. I open my eyes under water, taste it . . . it's like making love after a long absence. The past feels real, unchanged, knowable, true. I find myself thinking about Thomas Wolfe's statement "You can't go home again" and Katherine Anne Porter's response much later: "Nonsense, that is the only place you can go. You go there all the time."

That night my mother, my sons, and I play hearts with a smiling seriousness. Owen, the youngest, wins, shooting the moon twice. It's midnight before the smell of pine needles and the soft music of insects lulls us to sleep. In the morning the shouts of children and the clink of horseshoes wake us. My eyes focus on the window above my head, cantilevered open by a birch branch. And the day begins—breakfast, a game of cards, a swim. In a six-horsepower boat we maneuver around the pond, shouting over the asthmatic roar of the engine. Under the causeway bridge and into Long Lake, past the old cabin, and out to the long island in the northwestern part of the lake, Ian steers the boat, taking the same pleasure in being captain that I did at his age. Owen sits in the bow, laughing as the spray covers him, as the boat bucks over the waves, as he bounces to make the ride even wilder.

As we return we seem to race against the sun that warms my back. I smell the familiar aroma of gasoline and reach my hand into the rushing water. The victory seems to be ours, making us jubilant as we careen across the lake through the wind and spray, and dock the boat at the old grocery store to pick up supplies for the cabin. Twenty minutes later, arms full of shopping bags, we search the dock for our boat, which has disappeared. In a few minutes the mystery is solved. Never hitched properly, the boat drifted away and someone secured it to another dock. Our confidence in our seamanship is diminished, but the exhilarating sense of a victory over time is still with me. After all, I was just as careless at twelve. Time hasn't changed that.

> *What a place to live, what a place to die and be*
> *buried in! There certainly men would live for-*
> *ever and laugh at death and at the grave.*
> —Henry David Thoreau

The Abenakis called it Dawnland, but where the name "Maine" originated remains a mystery—perhaps from a province in France or maybe from a description of the island-studded shoreline. But as far back as the old timers can remember the slogan "Vacationland" has been attached to the state. John Smith, one of America's first public relations people, may have started the promotion when he wrote about Maine in his *Description of New England*: "Of all the foure parts of the world that I have seene not inhabited, could I have but meanes to transport a colonie, I would rather live here than any where." Of course, Smith was not the first European to be taken with the sight of Maine. Some historians believe Leif Ericson landed briefly there in 1000 A.D. as he sailed south from Canada. Probably, though, Sebastian Cabot, in 1498, was the first European to visit the coast of Maine. He was looking for the gold and silks of Asia, and it must have been a disappointment to bring back news of pine forests and codfish, instead. In 1605 George Waymouth led an expedition to Maine, but rather than settling the rocky shores, he satisfied himself with kidnapping a few natives and returning to England. In 1607, one hundred and twenty men settled in Maine but deep snows and frigid winters cut short the adventure. The French and English fought over the area, and eventually it became a part of the Massachusetts territory until it attained statehood in 1820.

By the nineteenth century shipbuilding and fishing were big industries. With its millions of acres of timberland, the region became a prime location for lumber companies. The mill towns and shipping ports can still be found, and the lumber companies own vast tracts of land in the northern part of the state, but tourism is the first industry in the land that Thoreau called an "archipelago of lakes . . . a wilderness of lakes." Its twenty-five hundred lakes and five thousand rivers and streams draw countless visitors.

In the nineteenth century, when industrialization struck the northeast, the summer tourists came—to Ogunquit, Kennebunkport, Bar Harbor, and to the lake regions. In many ways, Maine is still the "territories." By some accounts, not much happens there, and that's why many people come—to escape from the cities where everything is happening: traffic, pollution, violent crime. Maine is the poorest of the New England states, with the lowest per capita income, but according to the Green Index it protects the environment and health of its citizens better than any state other than Oregon. Perhaps it still resembles the landscape Sarah Orne Jewett celebrated in her books—villages, farms, seaports, the modest triumphs and pleasures of country life. It's still a rural state, with about thirty-three people per square mile, offering the kind of uninhabited spaces one can imagine only in the West. Portland, the largest city, has about one hundred thousand people.

I spend the day in the Naples Historical Society discussing these facts and the character of the state and the town with Beatrice Mitchell, the curator, and her grandson Chris Larsen, who has stopped by for a long morning chat. The historical society is in an old barn (Beatrice says "baaa n") that might very well hold a lot of stories in its musty rafters. Between Beatrice, who is eighty-seven, and Chris, who is twenty-three, there is no generation gap. Their views of the world sound as similar as their accents.

Their two voices rise up indistinguishably, a perfect harmony, in the story they tell. Like much of Maine, Naples began as a farming community, then became home to lumbering and grist mill operations. In the late 1800s summer boarding places began to spring up, and tourists would ride to Portland and Sebago Lake Station on the trains, then take the steamboats up to Naples.

Once or twice Beatrice slips back, referring to Long Lake as Wyonegonic, its old Indian name.

She speaks of George Peirce, the first white settler in Naples, as if she knew him personally. He died in 1801. For her Naples is still the old grist mills and canal boats. And although a quarter of a century has not changed the town in many significant ways that I can see, Beatrice is stunned by the transformations. "This used to be such a neighborly town," she says. "When I was a girl there was a wooden causeway across the connection between Brandy Pond and Long Lake. I'd walk across and say hello to everyone I passed. And know them all! There were a few hundred residents then. Now there are three thousand. We didn't even have electricity until 1921." I believe even now she would be willing to trade refrigerators and televisions for the virtues of the past she feels slipping from her grasp.

Her grandson Chris would, too. A college graduate, Chris refinishes furniture but is out of work. There aren't enough jobs in the area, but he won't leave it. "I'll move farther into the woods," he says, "but I will never leave." Like his grandmother, he has no desire to live in the modern world, at least not the way it is defined in New York or Los Angeles or even Portland. He'd rather sit back and contemplate bygone days in the historical society, waiting for his next encounter with the past—stripping and sanding an antique, bringing it back to life.

Out of curiosity I ask about famous former residents, or, better yet, notorious ones, but neither of them can think of any. So I ask about scandalous bits of history, crimes, murders, but after about five minutes of questioning they seem genuinely embarrassed that they can't recall even one respectable horror story. That is, until Beatrice sighs in relief and summarizes a recent piece of local news—a thirty-five-year-old man, a drifter of sorts, was recently arrested for poisoning a deep well at the Causeway Marina in town. He had been renting rooms there, gotten evicted, and with a Snopes-like sense of revenge had poured creosote, paint thinner, and motor oil into the well. Three people had gotten sick.

After contemplating two centuries of Naples history, Beatrice and Chris agreed that this was the most gruesome story to tell. And, as if to add a touch to the horror, Beatrice starts to talk about the Songo River, described by residents as the crookedest river in the world, and the frightening behavior that had occurred there in recent years. "Your life wasn't worth a nickel on the river, you know," Beatrice says. "The devils would go down there and race their boats!"

That night I while away a few hours reading Robert Dingley's history of Naples. Filled with bills of fare from steamboats, blurred photographs, school budgets, lists of prominent families—a biblical recounting of Ezekiels and Jedediahs—an occasional anecdote or a story about a boat race, the book is a compendium of modest triumphs and simple pleasures. It would be worthy of Sarah Orne Jewett if the writing were not unremittingly dull and often acrobatically ungrammatical. But the story left unwritten in the book, the one whispered between the lines, is about a time of innocence.

> *. . . from then on none of us ever thought there*
> *was any place in the world like that lake in*
> *Maine. We returned summer after summer.*
>
> —E. B. White

The rest of the week my mother, sons, and I spend with my sister Ginny and her husband Ray. It's like a summer thirty years ago, all card-playing, swimming, teasing, and laughter. We stroll through town, play video games, lick ice cream cones, and watch the boat lights sparkle on the lake. In the mornings Ray teaches me to play golf. He's old enough to act like an older brother, even a father, patiently showing me the proper grip and swing, smiling with me at my clumsiness. With my sons, too, he is like a father, jostling and hugging them, tousling their hair. The six of us are a family, and best of all there is no Bronx, no Brother Boniface, no cramped apartment, to return to in a few days. On our last night in Naples, on our way to the Lobster Pound, my sister sings in an angel's voice:

THE PAST

> With someone like you
> a pal so good and true
> I'd like to leave it all behind . . .

And, without saying anything, we all know we have.

Then the day of departure arrives, and once again it's like that last day of summer. I remember leaving Naples in late August or early September each year, driving east on 302, past the cemetery, the post office, Irving's Grocery, the center of town. I remember each building and boat, the stillness of the air, the emptiness of the main streets. But most of all I recall sitting in the back seat of that 1951 Ford with my sister, both of us crying as we squinted through tears into the rearview mirror at Tippy, the loping, determined dog who loved us, chasing our car through town and toward the highway.

The Bronx/Maine

CHAPTER 2

GEORGIA

> . . . the extent of the change and the break be-
> tween the Old South that was and the South of
> our time has been vastly exaggerated.
> —W. J. Cash, *The Mind of the South*

> I was coming to see that facts carry a traveler
> only so far: at last he must penetrate the land by
> a different means, for to know a place in any real
> and lasting way is sooner or later to dream it.
> —William Least Heat-Moon,
> *Prairy Earth*

I lived in La Grange, Georgia, for six years. I left over
three years ago but still see it rising like mist off a scum-
filmed pond. It comes back in my dreams.

My dreams about La Grange, with slight variations,
always have the same simple plot. I am forced to return
there to live. I once again work at the small college of

fewer than one thousand students that is placed delicately on a hill in the heart of the city, a town of slightly more than twenty-five thousand people. I'm not sure why I'm there or how I came to return. As happens in dreams, things seem distorted but oddly familiar. I recognize my house, the oak-shaded streets, neighbors' faces, colleagues. However, flickering shadows stretch over each scene, each face. And a hollow feeling of loneliness rushes through me like an unexpected and chilling wind. The wind turns into a hot knife when I think of my children—one of my sons—going to school there, going off on a school bus, perhaps, to the airless corridors of the junior high school on the shack-lined Render Street. Usually, at about this point in the dream, as I watch one of my children disappear down the street, I wake up in a cold sweat and look around my bedroom long enough to assure myself that I'm still in Virginia Beach, which seems no more southern than a suburb of Phoenix, and that no quirk of fate has transported me back to Troup County, Georgia.

This recurrent dream is not difficult to interpret. I have little desire to return to La Grange, Georgia, although there were many sweet and decent people there and a few good friends, as well. I feel that my children are better off in Virginia Beach, which, despite the miasmic suburban sprawl, offers worlds beyond the provincialism of small-town Georgia. But our six years there were an introduction to the South, a region that had previously been for me the stuff of stories—the words in Faulkner and Welty and O'Connor or the images in movies and televisions.

> *For it was he [Sir Walter Scott] that created rank and caste down here, and also reverence for rank and caste, and pride and pleasure in them.*
> —Mark Twain, *Life on the Mississippi*

> *The trouble is that my grandfather set more store by Sir Walter Scott than he did by Thomas More.*
> —Walker Percy, *Love in the Ruins*

> *One had to have castes.*
> —Theodore Dreiser, *An American Tragedy*

A few weeks after we moved to La Grange, my sons and I rode our bikes along the back streets of town and came upon a dirt road off one of the main streets. There was no sign but I knew it was called Redline Alley. I never found out where the name came from, but it seemed as if the road had been redlined by the town, marked off the list of acceptable streets. The main thoroughfare, Country Club Road, was paved, and houses perched like modified Monticellos on the hills running alongside it. Redline Alley was rutted and reminiscent of the past. On a map of La Grange, bordered by ads for Vote America, Milliken and Company, and Ideal Cleaners, Redline Alley ran barely a quarter of an inch, the lines running into unnamed space, as if the road just faded away.

In a sense that's exactly what it did, opening narrowly like an afterthought and drifting off into nowhere. We rode our bikes down Redline Alley, our tires spitting dust and stones, past the unpainted shacks balanced precariously on cinder blocks, until we came to the wire fence that separated those who lived in that world from the residents of the Callaway estate. Other than the flimsy fence only a softly sloping valley with a runnel of water trickling through it acted as a boundary between the wealthy and the impoverished. At the time, I stood there, one leg over the fence, and took in the scene, but it was some time later that I came to see it as typical of the South—the columned mansion with its terra-cotta roof and the frail shacks awkwardly united in the same field of vision. It was only later that I came to feel that I had come upon the true heart of Dixie, a strange tension between ideals and reality.

In those six years I found the true South to be a crucible of contradictions, but one thing is certain: the South still exists. As the North Carolina sociologist John Shelton Reed says, "Although many of the most dramatic cultural differences between North and South have been decreasing . . . an accumulating body of research suggests that it is easy to overestimate the extent of cultural convergence, and to underestimate the autonomy of southern culture." Reed makes it clear that his research points out that southerners are still different from other Americans, "that they are as different now as they have been at any time in the recent past." Not even industrial developments and urbanization have banished what he calls "the personality of the South." Despite contrary reports, the region hasn't been totally "losangelized" into malls and subdivisions.

Of course, there are malls and subdivisions, by my count far too many, but much of the character of the South—its geography and people—has stayed the same. During my six years in Georgia I used La Grange as a base to explore not only that state but North Carolina, South Carolina, Alabama, and parts of Louisiana, Mississippi, and Tennessee, as well. The South, I came to realize, is a separate country, attached to the United States but with its own history, language, culture, and set of values.

Much of the South is still rural. There is no megalopolis like the one that stretches from Philadelphia to Boston in the North. There are cities like Atlanta, holding the skyline with copper and glass, their roots twisting and stretching out in highways toward one treeless subdivision after another, but in many towns in the South, the piney woods are only a few miles beyond the city limits. This is especially true in small cities like La Grange. A few minutes' car drive and the city disappears. Atlanta is sixty miles to the north, Columbus forty to the south, the backwoods of Alabama to the west, and to the east there is nothing between La Grange and Savannah but back roads, Macon, and small towns that are in your rearview mirror before you notice them. As the poet James Seay has suggested, the land of bear hunts has become a nation of bass boats, but "there are still woods and uncrowded spaces in the South suitable for the outdoor life." What you find in a place like La Grange is that many of your neighbors own guns, that despite the Sunbelt image more people probably own shotguns than golf clubs, that many hunt and fish, and that there may be more pickup trucks per capita than in any other region in the country. If you drive out far enough on some country roads, you may still find those people Harry Crews describes in *A Childhood: The Biography of a Place*: "Tired people savaged by long years of scratching in soil already worn out before they were born."

And, again, despite the warm, cozy Madison Avenue images of the New South, dotted with golf courses and man-made lakes, the cold reality of poverty is pervasive. The deeper one penetrates the region, past the surfaces of expanding cities, the more readily the squalor shows its pockmarked face. Deeper into Dixie still generally means farther down the ladder of per capita income. It means lower teachers' salaries, less rigorous education. The pictures are similar to those in James Agee's and Walker Evans's *Let Us Now Praise Famous Men*. Drive out of La Grange on Hamilton Road, for instance, and you run a gauntlet of sad dwellings and rusting machinery. On the porches sit the hollow-cheeked, vacant-eyed victims of poverty, mostly blacks, looking like snapshots from the past. The unpainted shacks often have no bathrooms and are crawling with vermin. In the winter they are tinderboxes heated by wood stoves; in the summer they are sweatboxes. Driving down Hamilton Road is like passing along a POW camp.

> . . . and there is always the silence. . . .
> —V. S. Naipaul, *A Turn in the South*

Although the war between the races in the South has become far less violent, it still exists, a cold war that sends a chill through the air. For instance, a few months before I left La Grange I overheard two people talking about a lynching that occurred in town around 1915. Out of curiosity I looked into the story but found myself caught up in another one, a murder that took place in 1940, a murder that had all the characteristics of a lynching but the rope. From everything I could gather it was the last mob execution in the area. But it was close enough to the present for many of my neighbors to recall the incident. For some reason, though, none of them seemed to remember.

The story is a simple one: an eighteen-year-old black man, called Austin Callaway in one paper and Tom Callaway in another, was arrested on Saturday, September 7, 1940, on a charge of "attempted attack on a white woman." The young man was taken from the jail by six masked white men early the next morning and brought out eight miles into the country. It's not difficult to imagine the young man's terror or his clear knowledge of what was to take place. It's quite likely that the six white men finished their business in time to get to church that morning. Callaway was found later that Sunday on a road sadly named Liberty Hill. He had seven bullets in him.

I've heard stories like this many times before. I was less surprised by the mob violence than I was by the ensuing silence. The *Atlanta Constitution* had a brief story on the murder, but the local paper, the *La Grange Daily News*, had an even shorter notice, more elliptical than the piece in the Atlanta paper and squirreled away on page six, next to announcements about Miss Emilie Cole's returning to her home in Atlanta after a two-week visit with Miss Mildred Whitley on Hill Street or Mrs. C. B. Wheeler's trip to Daytona Beach, Florida.

It was now 1988, nearly fifty years after the murder, but few who were able to talk about the incident were willing to discuss it. The whites who had lived in La Grange all their lives and were old enough to remember it said they couldn't recall. The blacks looked trapped when I asked them. Mary Howell, a black woman who has lived her entire eighty years in La Grange, said, "The story just disappeared. It just went on its way, just like the wind blows something around a corner." Her husband, Joe Howell, said that nobody ever knew the real facts of the story, that back then "they" weren't interested in facts. But Howell remembers: they called it an attempted rape but some people whispered it was just an argument over how much Callaway was supposed to be paid for some yard work. He spoke too loudly, may have even dared to touch a white woman. According to Howell, Lamon Hand, a black man who was in the vicinity of the crime, was forced by the deputies to help them search for Callaway. Supposedly Hand captured Callaway on Boulevard Street, a few blocks from where the "attempted rape" occurred on Alford Street. "Back then," Joe said, "they did to colored folks any way they wanted."

But Joe doesn't say too much, for he's convinced that things haven't changed drastically in half a century. He may be right: the silence may just have gotten louder. I did all of my research at the Coleman Library in La Grange, a library that was part of the Callaway Education Association. The connection between Tom Callaway's story and the Callaway Education Association is cruelly ironic. As far as I could find there was no biological relationship between the murdered black man and the white millionaire mill owner who founded the CEA. But there is a connection. The CEA is a members-only club, a euphemism for whites only.* I am

*Since writing this chapter, I have learned that the CEA has given its recreation facilities to La Grange College, thus levelling one of the last prominent institutional racial barriers in the town.

white and although it shames me to admit it, I joined the CEA so that my children could use the pool, tennis courts, gymnasium; so that they could learn a musical instrument; so that they could take arts and crafts classes. I was part of the silence, allowing myself to believe that it wasn't a closed club, just an organization that wanted to meet its new members. I lied to myself and joined. Therefore, I had access to the books and records in the library, to the scraps of history that make up Tom Callaway's death. A black man or woman would not be able to search through the same files, although they would be able to clean the bathrooms or mow the grass. The Supreme Court decision of 1954 did not change the story here. As Joe Howell said, "Some things ain't never going to change."

The situation for blacks in La Grange and towns like it in the South is certainly different from what it was fifty years ago—but not as different, perhaps, as many of us would think. The town, like many in the South, is still divided, segregated into neatly colored coordinates, blacks on one side of the tracks and whites on the other. Occasionally poor whites live near or even in black neighborhoods, but rarely does the reverse occur. Towns such as La Grange have no black middle class. They barely have a white one. It is the mansion or the shack, a plantation society that refuses to allow the old stereotypes to die. I remember, for instance, driving my son Ian to the elementary school a few mornings each week. Whenever I did, I encountered the same cleaning

Georgia

man who shuffled along sweeping the halls and in response to my "Hello, how are you this morning?" or any other greeting would say, "Yes, suh, yes, suh," duck his head and amble along like Stepin' Fetchit. He reminded me of John Blassingame's description of the slave in the South, always reacting to cues from whites. "He [the slave] had to be a lifelong student of the white man's moods, ideas, and actions," Blassingame wrote, "and then conduct himself according to the changes in the white man's behavior." As Joe Howell had said, some things in La Grange had not changed much at all. There were still the "mammys" who cared for white children and the fifty-year-old "boys" who did yard work for many of my neighbors. The suburban dream was still mainly for whites.

As Bertram Wyatt-Brown in his remarkable book *Southern Honor* suggests, the South was a tribal community. It remains so today. There is a subtle relationship, Wyatt-Brown claims, among primal honor and the Stoic-Christian system and gentility. The notion of primal honor can still be heard in the intonations of southern senators like Robert Byrd or in the rhetoric of some southern lawyers, but generally honor has been transmuted into gentility, a strange dance of rituals and manners in the South. It seems true that, as Paul B. Escott has analyzed the situation, "courtesy, tact, and indirection helped a deeply divided society to function, and they still ease social intercourse today."

When I walked into my first college classroom in the South as an instructor I was taken off balance. In Vermont, where I had come from, none of the students called me "sir." And none of the young women dressed so well for class. In Vermont, as far as I could tell, none of the young women dressed so well for dates. This formality was part of the southern code of manners, a system of accepted practices, code words, gestures, and patterns that allowed members of the various levels of the caste system to negotiate the same streets and byways. The code determines everything from the formulaic "yes, suh" to a careful observation of titles, doctor or professor or reverend. Rank and caste are scrupulously respected. There are, as Flannery O'Connor observed, "fierce and fading manners" in such places as Georgia.

But the South is tribal in other ways, as well. There is a sense of locality in most southern towns, a loyalty to place. Families stay where they were born. Sons and daughters may go off to the universities at Chapel Hill or Tuscaloosa or Auburn, but most often they return home. There is a sense of history, of family, of a shared past. And even though there is an immediate friendliness in most southern towns, the inner circle of the tribe, the real center, is nearly impossible for a stranger, particularly a northerner, to enter. When my family and I moved to La Grange, we had visitors at our door for two weeks straight, bearing smiles and soft drawls and sweet potato pies. But in six years, few friendships got beyond the smiles. And when we left mainly silence followed us.

So finally the South I encountered was entangled in contradictions. Much of its comedy—from William Byrd and Augustus Baldwin Longstreet to Erskine Caldwell and William Faulkner to Flannery O'Connor, Lee Smith, Clyde Edgerton, and Harry Crews—sprang from paradox. The South is rife with ignorance but capable of eloquent talk; it is a place of easy smiles but narrow prejudices, violence and fundamentalist religion, formal attire and hunting caps, poverty but great pride. It's not easy to get a fix on such a geography. Donald Davidson, in his essay "Still Rebels, Still Yankees," said that the Georgia landscape offered a "serene repose that lulled a man out of all need of conscience." It was a land, as he suggested, of confusing opposites. The Georgian, he said, "remembered the faith and hankered after the fleshpots at the same time." La Grange had its fair share of adultery, but on Sunday mornings at eleven the streets were clear and the churches were full. As Davidson wrote, industrialism in the South "piled ugliness upon wreckage and threw the old arrangements out of kilter. The United Daughters of the Confederacy and the Kiwanis Club flourished side by side. Mule wagons and automobiles . . . aristocratic pride and backwoods independence disproved the axiom that two bodies cannot occupy the same space." In the face of such contradictions, the Georgian, according to Davidson, lived life horizontally: "You never crossed a bridge until you came to it—and maybe not then."

As I sit here examining the 1986 chamber of commerce map of La Grange I realize how confusing these intersecting lines can be. In the left-hand bottom square of the map, the chamber of commerce, along with the company that printed it, offers a paragraph releasing them from any responsibility to accuracy: "The information in this map was gathered and processed to ensure maximum accuracy, however, neither the La Grange Chamber of Commerce nor Commerce Productions Guarantee the correctness of all information nor the absense of errors and omissions." And, who knows, outside of a problem with capitalization, a comma splice, and a spelling error, maybe they got the rest right.

The history of La Grange has its own brand of contradictions. The city began as a small county seat in 1828, named in honor of the Marquis de Lafayette because he reportedly said that western Georgia reminded him of his French country estate, "La Grange." In nineteenth-century frontier Georgia, county seats were focal points for settlements, for the opening of the frontier. La Grange occupied a central place on the western frontier, on one of the main Indian highways that ran east-west through the territory. On these roads and others the whites swarmed in, pushing the Indians out by force or through legal maneuvering. Guilford Gilder, a nearby tavern owner, and John Williams, a local merchant, served as administrators for the Indian lands. They manipulated settlements, delayed sales, and bought enough land at bargain prices to build private fortunes and amass over four thousand acres. Meanwhile, the same old story between white man and Indian repeated itself, and by 1836 most of the Indians were gone. By 1840 there were over ten thousand settlers in Troup County.

The Methodist churches came soon after, and eventually La Grange became the religious center in the county. For many settlers it was the promised land in more ways than one. As Forrest Clark Johnson, the La Grange historian, speaking with a publicist's intonation, says, "There were few sections of Georgia with more fertile acreage. Streams and springs were pure and plentiful. The climate was pleasant and healthy. The forests were magnificent. Besides granite, limestone and other suitable building rock abounded, but did not hinder farming. Troup also had amethyst, tourmaline, and a trace of gold. The soil was perfect for all grains. Wheat, corn, barley, and rye prospered but cotton was the undisputed monarch of crops." By 1860 Troup County was the fourth wealthiest in the state. Johnson describes antebellum La Grange as a "top-heavy" society, with many slaves and no discernible white lower class. In this respect modern La Grange appears not to have changed all that much.

In 1840, 83 percent of the white families in La Grange owned slaves. By 1860, 74 percent of the town were blacks. In that same year the average number of slaves owned by white families was twenty-four. As Johnson says, "Wealth, created by blacks, directed by whites, was the cornerstone of La Grange's uniqueness. It generated gracious living and the ability to support institutions that further enhanced the town's reputation." Johnson goes on to say that the residents of the town "were secure with what they had obtained and interested only in maintaining it." Maintaining the status quo became an industry, of sorts, and La Grange did an admirable job keeping radical change at bay. Not even the march of Sherman's forces affected it too much. Perhaps luckily for the town, the Union commander of the forces that marched through the area in 1865 was Colonel La Grange, and he spared the homes, either out of eponymous empathy or chivalric sympathy when he was met by a group of local women at the city line.

So the town survived the war and endured Reconstruction. La Grange Female Academy, which had become La Grange College in the middle of the nineteenth century, sprung back to life. Free blacks were little more than slaves during this period. The whites still owned the land but because of the war they could not pay wages. Blacks were paid with housing, clothing, and food. Slavery became feudalism. Capitalists became kings. Blacks and poor whites were serfs. In 1888 the owners of La Grange Oil and Manufacturing Company converted their plant into the town's first textile mill, and a new aristocracy arose. A second factory, Dixie Mills, was organized, then faltered, and was eventually saved by Fuller Earle Callaway, who became a legend in La Grange. The outline of his story of heroic capitalism is known by every schoolchild in the county. As a young boy he sold merchandise to farm families, walking for miles and saving every penny. By the time he was fourteen he worked in a local clothing store. Within four years he had accumulated enough money to open his own store. In his twenties he was doing a mail-order business in thirty-six states, and before he was twenty-five he was part owner of one of the largest mills in the county. By thirty he was one of the wealthiest men in the state. It's a tale straight out of Horatio Alger.

With Callaway's help mill villages sprung up around the town. Plantation paternalism was revised into industrial paternalism. Callaway and other mill owners provided houses, schools, stores, churches, and recreational facilities for their workers. Mill villages were like plantations, down to the cotton that fogged the air, clinging to the workers and giving them the name "lintheads."

According to Forrest Johnson, La Grange was "one of the few places where the legendary 'Old South' existed." From cotton plantations to cotton mills, from frontier county seat to distant exurb of Atlanta, things had not changed all that much.

*There are only two or three human stories, and
they go on repeating themselves as fiercely as if
they had never happened before.*

—Willa Cather, *O Pioneers*

*There's some things even a Snopes won't do. I
don't know just exactly what they are, but they's
some somewhere.*

William Faulkner, *The Hamlet*

It was dusk by the time big Mac and I began walking
back through the woods towards his pickup truck. We
had spent the day trekking through the bottomlands and
across hilly pastures on the hundreds of acres his father
had left to him and his brother, profits from the gasoline
business. Occasionally, Mac would stop, as if an important idea had occurred to him, pull the .38 revolver from
his hip, and shoot at a tree. "Just to keep in practice,"
he'd say. "There's a lot of crazy niggers and northerners
in Troup County these days."

I had met Mac a few months before, and even though
I had known some unusual characters in New York City
and Vermont, he seemed like no one I had ever met. I
first saw him standing outside a new townhouse on the
end of my street. He was leaning against the hood of his
white Ford truck. His silver Mercedes was parked a few
feet behind it. He was only about six feet tall, but he
seemed much taller. The expanding belly, the jowls, the
thick arms—all made him seem to be a bigger man than

he actually was. He wore jeans, a white shirt, dark green alligator boots, and a Rolex that was as heavy as his Georgia accent. When he talked, his voice was always louder than you were expecting it to be, as if he believed there were a connection between decibels and insights. When he saw me, he shouted, "I'm Ken McDaniels. What kind of niggers live in this neighborhood?" His sister lived down the block, so he was just making conversation, not inquiring about the value of his recent real estate purchase, but my northern accent slowed him down a little. He didn't use the word "nigger" again for a few weeks.

As I got to know him, I didn't get to like him more, although he was hard to truly dislike, but I became more curious about him. The more time I spent with him, the more he seemed a caricature of the New South, a redneck with a Mercedes.

His family had become wealthy in the gasoline business. His father had made the McDaniels name one of the three or four most important in the town, and he had built a blindingly white southern mansion with stately columns on a hillside on the outskirts of the city. The father had been dead for a number of years, but the mother continued in robust and elegant good health, as many southern women did after their husbands died. A statuesque, grey-haired aristocrat, she appeared to thrive in her widowhood, like a matron in a Walker Percy novel. Mac's younger brother had gone to Yale for a law degree and Harvard for an M.B.A. Mac had gone to Hogansville High School, in a town that wasn't even a dot on most maps. It was a town that would be remembered by some for the one professional football player who grew up there. A few others would remember the poem by James Seay, "It All Comes Together Outside the Restroom in Hogansville." In it, Seay describes a hole cut into the bathroom wall of J. D. Hines's Garage in Hogansville, a hole cut for the purpose of some Snopesian voyeurism, but the poet takes the opportunity to look out into the world: "The interstate to Atlanta was wide open. / I wanted a different life. / So did J. D. Hines. So did the voice on the radio. / So did the man or woman / who made the hole. . . ." But Mac didn't. He didn't want anything more than Troup County. He really didn't even know what to do with the money he made after leaving the sheriff's department. He always carried a thick roll of bills, fifties and hundreds, like a mobster in an old film. He bought a bass boat, the best bourbon, and expensive watches, but a jon boat and a Timex would have served him as well. And he knew it.

He was loud and generous, peeling a thin layer of fifties off the fold of bills he took from his pocket, and always paying for everyone, anyone, saying, "Bidness is good. Put your damn money away." But his generosity was linked to his bigotry, and I began to feel awkward and ungrateful that I couldn't smile at his jokes or become enthusiastic about his narrow interests. Troup County, for him, was Eden—few Jews, "niggers" in their place, good fishing. His foreign policy consisted of two ideas: keep 'em out and nuke 'em. This kept things simple and left little room for discussion. For literature he read the newspaper, and for art he watched his favorite actor and film, Marlon Brando in *One-Eyed Jacks*. For entertainment he discussed sex or farting.

When I first met him, I was new to the South, and he was an emissary from this strange land. I was mesmerized: he was vulgar and generous, bigoted and sensitive to the smallest slights, laughing and moody, gregarious, lonely, simple, complicated, crude, and courtly. For a few months he became for me the South. So for a while I spent some time with him—on bass boats in the muddy orange waters of West Point Lake, fishing for catfish and keeping an eye out for tree stumps. We roamed the woods, drank some Wild Turkey on his back porch, and ate barbecue at his favorite places.

The night we returned from walking his country land we stopped by his warehouse to pick up some papers. There, pacing in front of the chainlink fence, was a black man about my age. He wore an oil-stained T-shirt, torn corduroy pants, and a pair of black high-top sneakers.

"Well, Jesus Christmas, Tennis Shoe, what the hell you doing here this time of night on a Saturday?" Mac asked, nudging me in the ribs. "This is Mr. Tennis Shoe," he said to me. "He keeps the riffraff away from the place when we're not around, don't you, Tennis Shoe?"

"Yes, suh, Mr. Mac, I certainly does," he said and,

with a barely noticeable movement of hips and feet, did a little shuffling dance. "Ain't nobody been here today," he sang, did a little moonwalk, and raised his hand backwards to meet the dollar bill Mac put into his palm like a runner passing off a baton in a relay race.

"Tennis Shoe is a good ol' boy, all right," Mac went on, taking out another dollar bill but holding it until the dance began again. Mac laughed as the dollar disappeared into the night, into the dark hand, but for an instant, no longer than it would take a runner to bobble a baton, Tennis Shoe lost his smile, his eyes narrowing into invisibility. Then he laughed, his smile curved out like the chipped blade of a scythe, and headed toward the package store.

I didn't see Mac after that, except to say hello in the street. The next year he moved out into the country, closer to his beginnings in Hogansville, and shortly after, I left Georgia. But Mac is still there. And Tennis Shoe. And probably that hole in the bathroom wall of J. D. Hines's garage, the hole that suggested to James Seay that "we devote ourselves to an image / we can't live with and try to kill / anything that suggests it could be otherwise."

Gordon Street, where I lived in La Grange, is still a quiet avenue lined by massive oaks and spreading dogwoods. There are magnolias and a few maples and a couple of tulip trees. In the summer it is a green strip. In the fall the leaves blanket the yards and streets, and the sound of leaves in the breeze and under foot is like the crisp, dry music of crickets. The winter is stripped and silent, but the spring blooms with careful combinations of colors.

It's the sort of street where small children ride big wheels or play in tree houses, and bigger children ride bikes or play touch football on the generous front lawns. It's small-town America, its surfaces reminiscent of a Norman Rockwell painting. It's the kind of neighborhood where parents leave their four-year-old unattended to play in the front yard, where it seems overly cautious to lock your doors when you go to the store—even, perhaps, unnecessary to worry when you go away on summer vacation.

Gordon Street felt safe, and it was. It was impossible to walk down the street without saying hello to half a dozen people. It was the kind of place David Goldfield describes as "a landscape of open windows and front porches framed by wisteria, crepe myrtle. . . . Soft summer evenings punctuated by the distant tinkling of a piano, the muffled clatter of dinner dishes. . . ." You knew all your neighbors. For that matter, you knew more than you wanted to know.

A few streets away lived the Phillipses, one of those families forming the aristocracy in La Grange under the supreme "big daddy," Fuller Callaway. The Phillips clan, unlike Callaway, had made its money in banking and speculating. Now, a wife, four daughters, three sons, seventeen grandchildren, thirteen dogs, twelve cats, and a flying squirrel were all ruled by James Phillips, the sixty-seven-year-old patriarch. He had been married forty-five years but had been faithful less than a quarter of that time. He believed, along with Woody Allen, that "people should mate for life, like pigeons . . . or Catholics," but Jim, Sr., had never seen a Woody Allen film—who cares what a little Jew from New York City has to say?—and although he was convinced that fidelity was for women, he knew the family must be held together.

Jim Phillips was tall and big boned, not handsome but charismatic. And rich. Nobody knew quite how much money he had, but it was enough to send his sons through law school, to buy everyone in his family a house, to purchase a bank for his sixty-second birthday, to continue ranching an unprofitable five-hundred-acre spread in the country, and to fall into and get out of scrapes with prostitutes and cocaine when it might have been more reasonable to have been playing shuffleboard in a Miami hotel. He reminded me of Faulkner's description of Will Varner in *The Hamlet*:

> [He] was the chief man of the country. He was the largest landholder and best supervisor in one county and Justice of the Peace in the next and election commissioner in both. . . . He was a farmer, a usurer, a veterinarian. . . . He owned most of the good land in the county and held mortgages on most of the rest. He owned the store and the cotton gin and the grist mill and blacksmith shop in the village proper and it was consid-

ered, to put it mildly, bad luck for a man to do his trading or gin his cotton or grind his meal or shoe his stock anywhere else.

Phillips was a man of this magnitude. His craziness fit the same proportions. He smoked his cigars, letting the ashes fall where they may. He expected those around him to pay attention. If he got angry at some remark at the dinner table, he was apt to throw a steak knife into the sheetrock, where it vibrated even after his anger subsided. He would curse his daughters in public, and expect his cousin, who was the town sheriff, to fix all his speeding tickets. One weekend he spent forty-eight hours chasing his wife around the town. She hid, like an underground slave, as he combed the streets in his yellow truck, a loaded shotgun on the seat next to his.

He didn't live with his wife, Margaret, and hadn't for about ten years. He bought her a small house in town and visited her a few times a week. She prayed for him, sometimes aloud as he sat at the kitchen table. She prayed, he drank. Sometimes he went off to Columbus to visit a woman who lived in a house he owned. Sometimes he stalked Margaret, pounding on the doors of his children's homes, demanding that he be allowed in to search.

The family took his money along with his moods. For the town his behavior was scandalous but not shocking. Southern towns are used to scandals, to bourbon-soaked professors who speak with the fiery rhetorical flourishes of Henry Clay in the morning but after five o'clock with the swollen-tongued dullness of a drunkard; to the poor-white beauty queen turned socialite who abandoned her just-born baby under the bleachers of the high school football stadium before a game one Saturday; to the kindly grandfather, his throat slit by his homosexual lover in the early morning hours before the school buses coughed around the corners.

Violence, sadness, and loneliness could be found beneath many of the Rockwellian colors on Gordon Street. There was a surface, as impermanent as a gesture, of friendliness and community, but it didn't seem to go very deep, nor did it last very long. In the pages of the chamber of commerce magazine that now lie in front of me, La Grange is filled with sunsets, warm colors, smiles. There are no photographs of Redline Alley or Render Street, but both are there, voiceless lines on the city map.

> *There was such speed in her little body,*
> *And such lightness in her footfall,*
> *It is no wonder her brown study*
> *Astonishes us all.*

>> —John Crowe Ransom,
>> "Bells for John Whiteside's Daughter"

She looked like a pretty child when she walked into my classroom at La Grange College. Her wrists were as thin as party ribbons, and her hair was the color of end-of-summer wheat. Her nose turned up slightly, under wide, wondering brown eyes. Her voice trilled in short bursts of excited speech.

But she wasn't a child—she was twenty-three years old, had already graduated from a prestigious southern college, and was taking courses to complete her requirements for a teaching certificate. Her life had not become what she had wanted. Her aspirations to be a poet were fading, and she entered La Grange, taking courses at the backwater college she had fled from a few years before. There, in her eyes, failure flickered. Beneath her gentle voice was an urgency. Occasionally, a flock of words would fly from her mouth like doves spooked by a footfall. Then she spoke rapidly, barely pausing for a breath, as if the sound of her voice were enough to hold back the confusion and fear.

In class she spoke often. She always had an opinion—on anything from verisimilitude to venereal disease. At first everyone listened. After a few weeks, only I did. The students had had enough. To them, her voice was pervasive, insistent, uncompromisingly present. She would not yield to silence—she saw it, perhaps, as death.

Her family was used to both success and failure. Her collection of brothers and sisters were drunkards and entrepreneurs, troubled artists or fervent Methodists. Her mother was a character who had faded from the stage like one of the disembodied women in a Tennessee

Williams play. Her father, a prominent gynecologist, made enough money to act as strangely as he wished, getting drunk at local parties and falling on top of his host's daughter or shooting holes in the swirled plaster ceiling of his dining room while he called his wife a bitch in three different languages, bits of the chandelier raining down on them like fairy dust. None of this, rumor or fact, dissuaded the women in town from paying visits to his office, as if his craziness at home assured his careful sanity at work.

From this world his youngest daughter emerged—pampered, ignored, frightened, amused, hungry. She needed to be something, to escape family, town, history, and in poetry she thought she had a chance to find out who she was, to discover—she hoped—that she didn't belong in La Grange. She had a talent, but not enough to satisfy her or the world. So she took literature courses and thought of teaching in the junior high school. It's difficult to imagine things working out for her, that her young students would gaze at her with rapt attention, because even her fellow students turned their eyes up and smiled when she began to speak. After some time, they whispered, then mocked her openly. I had no alternative but to tell her that some silence was necessary. She wanted to be something, she told me, but as she looked around La Grange she couldn't find what that was. So she felt lost and couldn't find the words to save herself.

Quietly, she remained in class. The other students

seemed pleased. Then one day she was gone. The semester ended, then the year, and I left Georgia.

It was about two years later that I received word that she was dead. I had known her only a few weeks, but someone called to tell me. She was found in her house in the mountains of North Carolina hidden in the closet, hanging from a beam. The house was silent, not a hum from the refrigerator or a faucet dripping. She had left no message at all.

> *The happiness of the South drove him wild with despair.*
> —Walker Percy, *The Last Gentleman*

> *The terror comes from piteousness, from good gone wrong and not knowing it, from Southern sweetness and cruelty, God why do I stay here . . . Better to live in New York City where life is simple, every man's your enemy, and you walk with your eyes straight ahead.*
> —Walker Percy, *Love in the Ruins*

So I ran from La Grange, escaping the stranglehold of southern gentility and eccentricity, the smiling faces at college tea parties, the entanglements of community, the caste system, the unabashed poverty, and the burdens of history, heading not for the territories but for the sprawling anonymity of the American urban-suburban nexus. I ended up in Virginia Beach, which seemed fitting, for as a boy growing up in New York City I had often dreamt of living by the ocean, close enough to see it from my window. For a year and a half, the time it took us to sell our house in Georgia, we rented a home on Oceanfront Avenue, with a view of the water from the second-floor porch.

Virginia Beach didn't resemble the real South any more than Miami Beach does. As far as I could tell it was just part of a geographical bit of sleight of hand. In Norfolk-Virginia Beach and the seven-city area that makes up the unrestrained growth in Hampton Roads, the military influence is strong, and the culture is as nomadic as any place in the United States. The taste of anonymity is as real as the salt in the water. Nevertheless, life on the beach, especially in the fall and winter, was much as I had imagined and hoped for. It was private and silent. No crowds sunbathing or swimming. A few surfers, maybe, and at times a hiker or two along the sand. But, generally, I felt the world was mine.

Most people love the beach, and there's a logical reason for it, especially for those of us who live in urban areas. Our vision is cluttered with cars, buildings, billboards, and traffic lights. This sort of world contrives against openness. The unwritten law seems to be that if there's a space it must be filled—a field with a subdivision, a vacant lot with a mini-mall. The developer has become a contemporary god. If there's a silence we feel compelled to shatter it. Radios blare, horns honk, people scream. Televisions and VCRs don't break down:

they die of exhaustion. For many, the outside world is just an extension of the media—and it's best to let walkmen and watchmen filter actual experience.

The beach in the fall and winter offers a silence and an openness. The ocean is rhythmic and soothing, a repetition of sound as soft as a pulse, a sound that washes away noise like the buzz of cicadas. Most of our shoreline has been built up with hotels and restaurants, but Robert Frost was right when he said, "The people along the sand / all turn and look one way. / They turn their back on the land. / They look at the sea all day." When we look out to sea, there is no clutter. Nor will there ever be. The ocean soothes and heals those of us blinded by the distractions bulldozed daily into our vision. It allows us to see. And even if, as Frost suggests, most of us can't look very far or very deep into the meaning of things, there's much to see on the beach on any given day.

A black-hooded tern may spread its narrow wings, straighten its forked tail and dive headlong into the sea. A cormorant may scoop a fish up into its expanding pouch and stretch its mighty wings to glide away just as a school of dolphins bursts from the water. During low tide, a line of overturned horseshoe crabs will lie like a squadron of abandoned, rusting tanks along the shore.

It is a beautiful, barren, lonely landscape. Any day can bring a surprise. The absolute openness compels attention, forces you to notice things you hadn't before. For instance, gulls are rather silly birds. In order to utter their squeaking caws, they scrunch up their necks like third-rate comedians imitating Ed Sullivan. The wind speaks in many voices, from a hushed whisper to a literal howl. It can calm the nerves or tear into the very clapboards of a house. The beach is filled with colors, more than just gray and blue—there are pinks and browns and silvers. Great spaces make us alert to small changes. At dusk at least five colors appear: the blue-green of the water, purple in the sky, flashes of orange from the setting sun—and within minutes everything turns light gray, then black.

So for that first year and a half away from La Grange, Georgia, we lived with the ocean in view, in a house my wife called "the lighthouse." We had plenty of privacy—probably because most of the homes were vacant, their wealthy owners off elsewhere, in warmer climes. Our three boys learned to play mostly with each other. Our community shrunk to the five of us.

In La Grange the streets were empty only on Sunday mornings when everyone was in one of the Baptist or Methodist churches. On the oceanfront in Virginia Beach, the streets were empty from late October until April. If we had eccentric neighbors we didn't know about them, any more than an apartment dweller in New York City knows the person who lives a few feet above him or next door. There were none of the restrictions of southern community, only freedom.

But, somehow, the freedom wasn't enough. We missed the sometimes jostling friendliness of some of our neighbors, the sound of voices calling from one back yard to another, the simple musical beauty of the southern tone, the wild and strange behavior and the stiff formality, twisting like two unyielding vines. We missed the human drama. A week before we left La Grange, our neighbors gave us a going-away party, which they videotaped. Watching that tape, as we have a number of times over the last few years, produces a strange longing and a pointed sense of loss. There was much about La Grange, and Georgia as a whole, that would always feel like a foreign land to me. What I regretted leaving behind was not La Grange or the South but a small town, perhaps *any* small town, with familiar faces and recognizable voices. Eventually we moved to the suburbs, the closest thing we could find to a compromise between a sometimes frigid northern anonymity and an occasionally stifling southern community. After all, we had just recently left Georgia and tomorrow would be another day.

CHAPTER 3

SAN FRANCISCO—
An Interlude

My dream goes out like sounds from a passing plane. . . .
— Patrick Smith, "Yawning Alone"

The night after Christmas 1991 the San Francisco sky I peer into from a plane window is the color of my wife's eyes, a slate blue that gets deeper as I stare. It's easy enough to get lost in those blue-eyed distances, memories flickering like lost stars. Twenty years ago, nearly the same day and hour, I flew back from New York City to San Francisco. Twenty-two years old, four months married, I soared above America at thirty thousand feet, sitting next to a young woman with a tangle of golden hair and the face of an angel. Now, though she sits at home, her image rises from the lights of the city and holds the present and past together in my mind.

V. S. Naipaul once said, "There is no landscape like the landscape of our childhood." But, of course, we all have many childhoods. The geography of first real love may be the most dramatically remembered landscape in anyone's past. Its sharp features and clear colors never fade. Memory triggers the rush of blood, the quickening pulse, the tightening flesh.

San Francisco is my first love. In 1971, right after I graduated from college and a few days after I got married, we drove across the country, found a cheap apartment on Ashby Avenue in Berkeley, and began graduate school at the University of San Francisco. That year was a dream, the promise of first love, and through some undeserved good luck the dream never turned its back on me. I've never lost faith in that promise, and for me the city has never lost its wild beauty.

In the early seventies, Berkeley and San Francisco were surely the land of golden dreams for many young people. Communes and protest against the war. LSD and Haight-Ashbury. Ginsberg, Kesey, and City Lights Bookstore. It was the West, as far as you could go. And in America it was still in heading west that you found yourself or got some idea of what it meant to be American.

San Francisco was the urban outpost where you could get away with anything, wear anything, smoke anything, drift aimlessly, be free. It was not unlike the nineteenth-century San Francisco that Doris Muscatine describes as "freewheeling, free-drinking, hard living," a place where the gold rush gamblers believed "the odds could turn spectacularly in their favor."

At twenty-two, roaming the breathtaking hills of San

Francisco with a woman who made my heart race more than the steep climbs, I felt as if I had been made that instant. The whole world seemed new, mysterious and unclaimed. I felt like an explorer among the residents of the city, who appeared to me to be similar to Muscatine's description of the original dark-skinned, naked San Franciscans—no bloody puberty rites, few weapons, little violence—the peaceful Costanoans. Those Costanoans, according to Muscatine, enjoyed dancing, sports, storytelling, drinking homemade beer, smoking tobacco, and liberal sexuality. Like Francis Drake four centuries before, I had landed in a safe harbor.

That year we hitchhiked across the Bay Bridge whenever our 1966 Pontiac Tempest broke down, which was often. We had little money for restaurants or theater, but food seemed to be the last thing we needed. The world was so full of other things. The streets provided a show—shopkeepers arguing in alleyways in Chinatown, poetry readings on the steps of Sproul Plaza, dancers, musicians, tourists, a teeming sea of faces. Life bubbled up around us faster than it could be recorded, but we had all the time in the world. There was never any rush as we strolled through Golden Gate Park, sat on the beach near Muir Woods, or drove dreaming past the mansions on Pacific Heights.

For me, then, San Francisco was always first love. In my mind the city will always have a strong breeze or a gentle rain. It never fully sheds a light fog, it's always slightly out of reach, always achingly beautiful, like a

San Francisco

young girl, all mystery and shy smiles and swelling flesh. It's sweet curving Victorian shapes, sensual hills, earthy smells from North Beach and Chinatown, it's small dusty grocery stores . . . it's the face of an angel seen through the mist.

> . . . *the past can change at any moment.*
> —Jorge Luis Borges, an interview

I was returning to San Francisco to interview job applicants at the Modern Language Association Convention. This meant I would be locked in a room at the Westin St. Francis Hotel for four days, staring at beige rugs, oatmeal-colored walls, wing-tip shoes, wool pants, and tweed jackets, as an apparently never-ending line of candidates talked of intertextuality and the new historicism for the allotted thirty minutes. Trapped in that elegant room, I could as readily have been in Des Moines, but I vowed to step into the city every chance I had.

First, I decided to look up a professor I had much admired during my graduate school days at the University of San Francisco. We had corresponded off and on over the years, and his voice in those letters reinforced my memories of him. In 1981 when my house burned down in Vermont, among the few books salvaged from the fire were some charred copies of his poetry. From 1971 to 1972, when I worked on my master's degree, he had been my mentor—maybe closer to hero. He had a pony tail and a long gray beard. He was calm, assured, philosophical. As poet, photographer, filmmaker, and teacher, he understood the world and responded to it creatively. He had a beautiful wife, seven children, a clear sense of his place in the world. The word "teacher" always brought his steady eyes and patient smile into my mind. When we studied the literature of the day, he became for us Brautigan and Kerouac and Cassady— only steadier, less suicidal.

As I stood waiting outside the elevator near the English Department at USF the doors opened and a man said, "Hello, Mike." I had to look twice before the voice registered. The man was about five-foot-six, his head and face shaved to a pink shine. A three-piece green-check suit fit a bit too snugly. This was my mentor, a shrunken, hairless imitation of my grand memory?

He had become a union representative. That accounted for the suit. Far Eastern religious philosophy explained the hair. Only the romanticizing of my memory made sense of his loss of stature. He had always been much shorter than I. As we talked for awhile I found out he had gotten divorced and remarried. He told me about some of the problems his children had getting through school. He talked about university politics. It didn't take me long to realize that he had not changed; he had always been short, faddish, perhaps a bit insecure, but also a generous listener, a courageous

San Francisco

73

teacher, an individual spirit. My perspective, as a student gazing up at the front of the room, had never allowed me to see him very clearly.

He had been an emblem of San Francisco for me back then, and my meeting with him made me wonder in what other ways my vision had been blurred by youth or the ensuing years. So, with the stolen moments I could manage from the daily interviews, I hunted through the city, looking for the truth of my own memories.

At first, twenty years hadn't seemed to change San Francisco all that much. The Transamerica Building still rose like a triangle of light against the night skyline. Kan's, by most accounts, remained the best restaurant in Chinatown. The cable cars, jammed with tourists and occasionally with Asian-American commuters, bells clanging, the acrid smell of metal heating against metal, continued to jerk up and down the hills between Market Street and Fisherman's Wharf. Lombard remained the crookedest street in the world, and San Francisco seemed the most walkable city on earth and one of the most handsome. Compared to New York City, it seemed safe, with fewer police, less anger. San Francisco, as one historian put it, had never taken itself quite as seriously as some eastern cities like Boston or Philadelphia.

Even the homeless sometimes have a teasing tone, "Hey, man, nice tie! Can you spare some change? No?

That's okay, I still like your tie." But no tone can alter the harsh reality or hide a community of beggars that wasn't this large twenty years ago. Poverty creeps insidiously up the affirming slopes of Powell Street. It reaches around Union Square, leans against the building, sits on the sidewalk, curls like a fetus in the doorways. An army of street people, their forces seeming to rise straight out of *The Grapes of Wrath*, cover the streets. A chorus of voices ring out on every corner—"Buy a paper. Help the homeless. Can you spare even fifteen cents so I can eat? Please help me—I'm sick." Most people walk by, staring rigidly ahead, eyes focused sharply on some far distant point as they angle into I. Magnin or Banana Republic.

The night before I leave, as I sit at a table in Victor's thirty-two floors above Union Square, the lights of San Francisco splayed out toward the bay where a few freighters float lazily in the darkness, a thin fog begins to blanket the streets. In Victor's waiters with French accents bow gracefully, and Chopin plays softly in the background while far below the people seem too small to be real. They are tiny shadows amid the street lights. But for a moment I imagine a shadow moving into the light and a face below turning up to meet my eyes; we recognize one another and soundlessly call each other's names.

That morning, as the plane leaves San Francisco, the sky once again is a heartening slate blue. There is a belt of orange strapped across the horizon. The western United States opens in a burst of vast space, populated only with ghostly images of people in wagons and trucks and cars heading west, leaving the past behind in a trail of dreams.

PART TWO

THE PRESENT

I am certain of nothing but the holiness of the heart's affections and the truth of the imagination—

—John Keats in a letter to a friend

. . . it is a knowledge that resides in the marrow of their bones, in the chambers of their hearts.

—Robert Coles, *The Call of Stories*

CHAPTER 4

NEW MEXICO / ARIZONA

I will tell you something about stories. . . .
They are all we have, you see,
all we have to fight off
illness and death.
You don't have anything
if you don't have the stories.
      Leslie Marmon Silko, *Ceremony*

He was back in Dine' Bike' yah, back. Between
the Sacred Mountains, and he felt easy—at
home in a remembered landscape.
      —Tony Hillerman, *The Ghostway*

Coyote's always out there waiting.
      —Tony Hillerman, *Coyote Waits*

Black Creek was bone dry. Bits of bleached red rock shone in the moonlight that splashed through an opening in the clouds. There was more humidity than usual, and a skein of sweat coiled down the side of the driver's neck. When the Navajo Tribal Police car that was working the graveyard shift made a left turn onto Mission Road, it rumbled over the cattle guard and stopped alongside the pickup truck overturned in the ditch. The only sounds in the still air were the occasional cracklings of the cooling engine. There was no sign of a driver or passengers.

After searching near the truck for a few minutes the two officers got back in their car and coasted slowly down the road, eyes scanning left and right. It was only a matter of seconds before they saw the man holding a rifle as if he intended to use it at any moment. He stood next to the eight-foot-high crucifix that rose into the pieces of moonlight and shadow under the cottonwood that partially hid the front of St. Michael's Mission from view. The police car drove slowly around the curve, the men inside following the barrel of the rifle from the corners of their eyes. The car turned left at the museum building and parked on the crest of the hill directly across from the mission. With their lights off they could see without easily being seen. Behind them was a dirt road and silence. In front the moonlight played drunkenly on the shapes in the mission garden. They called for backup.

When Sgt. Whitegoat got the call he was at the station staring absently at the eye of sandstone that gave Window Rock its name. By the time he arrived at the mission the man was gone from the front of the building.

Whitegoat got out of the car and walked to the bottom of the front steps, glancing briefly through the shadows at Jesus' sad eyes before he climbed back into the Tribal Police Chevy Blazer and drove into the parking area behind the church.

The moon had fallen behind some clouds, and darkness had slid in with nightmarish suddenness. Whitegoat's partner covered him from the rectory as he went up behind the church. Unholstering his pistol, he walked into the courtyard and checked each parked car, shining his flashlight into the back seats and flinching at the shapes made by old blankets or coats. Slowly, he worked his way along the edge of the stone building until he came to an outside stairway. He positioned himself behind it, using it as a shield, and waited.

It didn't take long. A middle-aged Navajo, swaying as he whispered to himself, came into the courtyard with a rifle cradled in his arms. He rested against the corner of the building under the overhanging terracotta, closing his eyes and leaning his head back like a fighter looking to regain his strength.

In that instant before his body reacted, Whitegoat thought, "He has a gun. Either he is going to kill me or I will shoot him. And I have a family to go home to." He turned on his flashlight and yelled, "Police officer— don't move!" But the man kept coming. Whitegoat repeated even louder, "Police officer—don't move!" The man lowered his rifle, but he kept staggering toward Whitegoat.

New Mexico/Arizona

Again Whitegoat told him to stop, to drop his weapon, but the man only stood unsteadily before him with empty eyes. Whitegoat said later that he felt no fear because he was in control of himself. "To be a person, to be a human being, is to know your weaknesses, to know yourself. I know what my fears are and I understand them."

So he stood there, gun pointed at the drunken Navajo, index finger tense against the trigger, and waited calmly for what was to come, to see if the "dark wind" that had entered the man had completely destroyed his judgment. The Navajo word for whiskey was *todilhil*, "water of darkness," but at times Navajos intentionally mispronounced it *todilhaal*, which meant "sucking in darkness."

Whitegoat watched the man, nearly drowning in the dark waters, and wondered if with some act of drunken stupidity he would try to drag him down too. The man was less than twenty feet away. This time Whitegoat said more softly, "Drop your gun. I don't want to shoot you." Although the man still seemed unable to comprehend the meaning of Whitegoat's words, he let the rifle slip to the ground. His arms hung loosely at his sides, his chin slumped against his chest.

The drunken sheepherder was taken into custody, the mystery of his actions explained by the waters of darkness. For Whitegoat the world was restored to light and beauty, to what the Navajos call *hozro*, a harmony with the environment.

This is Tony Hillerman's country, the Navajo Reservation, mainly in Arizona and New Mexico but with a small portion in Utah as well, a nation of twenty-five thousand square miles, larger than West Virginia, nearly as large as all of New England but with a population of little more than 150,000. It's a landscape that Tony Hillerman has brought to dramatic life in his mystery novels, which focus on Jim Chee and Joe Leaphorn, two Navajo Tribal Police officers. Like Chee and Leaphorn, Sgt. Wally Whitegoat has many times encountered a sort of witchcraft on the reservation, a form of evil similar to that found by Hillerman's heroes: "He [Jim Chee] saw it in people who had turned deliberately and with malice from the beauty of the Navajo Way and embraced the evil that was its opposite. He saw it every day he worked as a policeman—in those who sold whiskey to children, in those who bought videocassette recorders while their relatives were hungry, in the knife fights in a Gallup alley, in the beaten wives and abandoned children."

Mystery is the lifeblood of Hillerman's fictions, but the land and the Navajo people are the heart of his work. Like Whitegoat, Hillerman searches not so much for answers to puzzles but rather a way of finding order and beauty in the world. His interest is in the spirit of the Navajo people and the severe, breathtaking quality of the land they live in. In Jim Chee and Joe Leaphorn, Hillerman has created representative, if idealized, Navajos and in the process offered one of the most vivid accounts of Native American life and culture in recent years.

> *I need only drive west from Shiprock and into*
> *that great emptiness to feel my spirit lift. And*
> *writing about it gives me the excuse to go.*
> —Tony Hillerman, *Talking Mysteries*

Hillerman himself is a bit of an anomaly. Born and raised in the tiny crossroads of Sacred Heart, Oklahoma, seventy miles southeast of Oklahoma City, Anthony Grove Hillerman is a self-declared redneck who grew up around Pottawatomie and Seminole Indians but who is often taken by unsuspecting readers to be a Navajo. He once said that he grew up like the Joads in Steinbeck's *The Grapes of Wrath*, the only difference being that the Joads had enough money to head to California. Hillerman's father ran a general store in a town that also had a filling station, a cotton gin, and a Catholic boarding school for girls that sat on a hill above the rest of the hamlet. Hillerman's parents sent him to that boarding school run by the Sisters of Mercy because it offered the best education around in a landscape of red clay and scrub oaks with the nearest library thirty-five miles away. The student body at the school was mostly girls and mainly Pottawatomies, and as Hillerman said of his experiences there with his friends, "The nuns forgave us for not being Pottawatomies, but they never forgave us for not being girls."

Because the town had no library, Hillerman's love of stories led him to order books from the mimeographed catalogue sent by the state library. With high anticipation, he would order *Captain Blood, Treasure Island*, or a Tom Swift adventure. In a few months a package would arrive with a note saying the librarian was sorry that the books he requested were not on the shelves; so instead the package contained books like *Modern Dairy Management* or the *History of the Masonic Order in Oklahoma*. Every once in a while something unusual would appear—*Beau Geste* or a novel by Arthur Upfield about the half-bred Australian aborigine police officer who was able to solve crimes in the desert outback because he understood the land and the people.

Upfield's influence lay dormant for over thirty years, but it never disappeared completely during Hillerman's days as a student, journalist, part-time public relations officer, or even as he wrote radio commercials for Cain's Better Coffee and Purina Pig Chow. It was his experiences growing up in the Oklahoma countryside and his love of reading that led him eventually by a long and circuitous route to write about the Navajos. In a *Newsweek* interview he spoke of sitting on the porch of his father's general store, watching and listening: "The WPA was working only half time, so all these guys were sitting around. So here came, maybe once a month, a strange car. Maybe it was clean, and a fairly new car, and it was just like a strange dog walking in. Everybody would freeze up, especially if the guy had a necktie on, or a suit. Even when I was a kid I was interested in the way people belong together."

Hillerman grew up as an outsider—a Catholic on the fringes of the Bible Belt, a white among Indians, a boy in a girls' school—and that sense of being a stranger in a strange land may have prodded him into writing. From the time he was a youngster his world had been divided, he once said, into "us" and "them," country boys and town boys. Finally, he felt more connected to his Pottawatomie neighbors, the Nonis and Harjos, than he did to the white boys from town. He grew up wearing work shoes and bib overalls. He was twenty-one years old before he made his first telephone call.

When he first met some Navajos, the Indian tribe that he has written about for the past twenty-five years, he immediately recognized kindred spirits. They too were country people, outsiders. "They're the bottom of the pecking order among tribes out here," he said. "They're the country bumpkins. And I've always identified with that." Just as he saw a strength and dignity in the people who gathered on his father's porch to tell stories, he found something in the Navajo culture that he understood and admired. A practicing Catholic and still a country boy at heart, Hillerman discovered in the Navajos a spirituality and rural wisdom, a value system reminiscent of his own growing up.

His first meeting with Navajos was in 1945. They were involved in a curing ceremony called the Enemy Way. Hillerman had just returned from serving in World

War II, a private first class with a Bronze Star, a Purple Heart, a Silver Star, a patch over one eye and a cane to help a damaged leg. He had survived being blown up in Alsace by a concussion mine, but both his legs were broken and he was temporarily blinded. As *Smithsonian Magazine* reported, "He was picked up by a stretcher crew. The lead stretcher-bearer was blown up, and Hillerman took another short flight. Two friends came up and got him on another stretcher and accidentally dropped him in a stream." He survived all that and was home on a sixty-day convalescent leave, working as a truck driver on the Navajo Reservation. He was fascinated by the ceremony that he observed. "Forty years later," he said, "I am still fascinated." As he has recently written, he needs only drive onto the reservation "into that great emptiness to feel my spirit lift."

It took him a quarter of a century to join his interest in the Navajo culture with his love of storytelling. After the service he took advantage of the G.I. Bill and studied journalism at the University of Oklahoma. He met Marie Unzner when he was a senior, and they were married in 1948. For the next fifteen years he worked as a journalist and editor, starting as a crime reporter on the Borger, Texas, *News Herald* and ending his career in 1962 as the executive editor of the Santa Fe *New Mexican*. Successful journalist, father of six (five of them adopted), and thirty-eight years old, Hillerman decided, like Hawthorne's Wakefield or a character in a Walker Percy novel, to start a new life. He wanted to be more than a journalist. "Working with facts, as a journalist must, is like working with marble," he said. "Truth has its beauty but it doesn't bend." So, in search of a more flexible form for his writing he took a part-time job as an assistant to the president of the University of New Mexico and began graduate school in the English Department.

He had read Eric Ambler, Ross Macdonald, Graham Greene, and Raymond Chandler and remembers thinking, "My God, you can do *anything* with this form." He tried his hand at it, and after a number of false starts he sent his work to an agent who advised him "to get rid of all the Indian stuff." Instead, he got another agent, but it was not until 1970, when he was forty-five years old, that his first novel, *The Blessing Way* (the title was changed by the publisher from Hillerman's intended *The Enemy Way*) saw print. By that time he was a professor of journalism at the University of New Mexico. After *The Blessing Way* the books came regularly—seventeen thus far, with ten in the Chee-Leaphorn series.

At first he had a small but loyal readership, described by Hillerman as "anthropologists and desert rats." He won an Edgar Award from the Mystery Writers of America in 1974 for *Dance Hall of the Dead*, and continued to entertain a modestly growing readership and a burgeoning number of admiring critics. In 1986, around the time he retired as a professor, *Skinwalkers* brought the youthful, intuitive Chee together with the older, more rational Leaphorn, and the combination put Hillerman on the best seller list, where he has been every year or so since that time. He received a contract from Harper and Row for over one million dollars, and Robert Redford bought the movie rights to all of his Navajo novels. *The Dark Wind* has proven to be a controversial story. Although the film was produced, it has yet to be released in America, and "that's fine with me" is Hillerman's reaction.

> *Your stories, like the stories our grandmother used to tell us, they make us feel good about being Navajos.*
> —Navajo librarian to Tony Hillerman

In one of Hillerman's mysteries detective Jim Chee recalls his key clan uncle's admonishing him to memorize places. "Settle your eyes on a place and learn it," he says. "See it under the snow, and when first grass is growing, and as the rain falls on it. Feel it and smell it, walk on it, touch the stories, and it will be with you forever. When you are far away, you can call it back. When you need it, it is there, in your mind." Hillerman's stories grow as naturally as sagebrush in the austere Navajo holy land. As Robin Winks wrote in *The New Republic*, "These books could exist nowhere else, they are authentic, and the resolutions grow out of the character of an entire people." All the mysteries turn upon the complex cultural life of the Navajos, all the stories are rooted in the arid soil of the reservation, all the solutions lead toward *hozro*, which Hillerman defines when he describes Leaphorn's motives in one of the stories: "The only goal for man was beauty, and that beauty was found only in harmony, and this harmony of nature was a matter of dazzling complexity. . . . Every cause has its effect. Every action its reaction. Thus one learned to live with evil by understanding it, by reading its cause. And thus one learned, gradually and methodically, if one was lucky, to always 'go in beauty,' to always look for the pattern, and to find it."

As a number of critics have pointed out, Hillerman's Navajo police heroes, Joe Leaphorn and Jim Chee, are perfectly suited to their roles as detectives. In Hillerman's first novel, *The Blessing Way*, he writes of the landscape, "In this silent darkness mystery seemed suddenly natural, almost rational." This may very well serve as an epigraph for all of his work. The very culture of the Navajo is fertile ground for the mystery writer. Leaphorn and Chee are reflections of the Navajo philosophy that suggests there is a pattern in all things. It is natural for Chee and Leaphorn to look for a design in any evidence they find. It is also an important part of Navajo culture to read the cause of evil and find a way of reestablishing beauty. The rational harmony that "Leaphorn's orderly soul" demands is representative of his culture at large. Among Navajos there is often an intense belief in the extra-rational, in witchcraft and the evil it produces.

THE PRESENT

Jim Chee explains this aspect of Navajo life to Mary Landon, the white schoolteacher, in *People of Darkness*: "The way it works with Navajos, witchcraft is the reversal of the Navajo Way. The way the Holy People taught us, the goal of life was *yo'zho*. No word for it in English. Sort of a combination of beauty/harmony, being in tune, going with the flow, feeling peaceful, all wrapped up in a single concept. Witchcraft is the reversal of this concept, basically. There's a mythology built up around it, of course. You get to be a witch by violating the basic taboos—killing a relative, incest, so forth. And you get certain powers. You can turn yourself into a dog or a wolf. You can fly. And you have the power to make people sick." As Chee goes on to explain, skinwalkers don't need motives for the evil they do, and a belief in witches and a fear of them lie at the heart of many of the tragedies Chee and Leaphorn confront. But witchcraft comes in many shapes, as Hillerman makes clear—in the drunken father, in the Navajo who has lost his sense of place, in the clash between Indian values and white ones. As one of Hillerman's friends said, "I've never met a Navajo who was skeptical about witchcraft." Witchcraft is the Navajo way of explaining evil. Characters like Chee and Leaphorn who are devoted to finding a pattern in puzzles symbolize a culture that feels a man must learn "to live with evil, by understanding it, by reading its causes," and that believes it is possible to achieve balance once the mysteries are solved.

Another key element in Hillerman's mysteries is the

landscape, which often seems to loom larger than the plot. As Jack Schneider has pointed out in *Southwest Review*, "Hillerman has removed the detective novel from the affluent drawing rooms of the earlier versions and the sleazy back streets of the modern school and placed it squarely in the midst of the hundreds of square miles of primal beauty and desolation that comprise the Navajo Reservation in Arizona and New Mexico." The significance of the land is another logical extension of Navajo culture. "For there is nothing more revered nor more loved by the Navajos than the land they call *Dinehtah*," historian Raymond Friday Locke has said. *Dinehtah* is a bit larger than the confines of the present reservation. It is bounded by the four sacred mountains that Navajo religion says was built by First Man to protect their homeland. It is protected on the north by the LaPlata Mountains in Colorado, on the east by the Sierra Blanca and Pelado Peaks, on the south by Mount Taylor and the Zuni Mountains, and on the west by the San Francisco Peaks outside of Flagstaff. The Navajo leader Barboncito explained to the American government in the nineteenth century that "when the Navajos were first created, four mountains and four rivers were pointed out to us, inside of which we should live." Outside of this sacred territory, Navajo religion says their people will never thrive. And just as the landscape is an integral part of Navajo life and metaphysics, it is a powerful part of Hillerman's work. The land takes on, as Jack Schneider describes it, "an active role in the novels, determining the nature of and the circumstances surrounding the crime, shaping and controlling the detection process itself, and dictating the terms of the resolution."

A sense of order and spiritual connection to the land, then, are both at the center of Navajo culture and driving forces in Hillerman's fictions. As Chee puts it, these are "things purely Navajo." And it is things purely Navajo that Hillerman has plumbed in his novels from the very beginning. In his first book he focused on the apparent murder of a young Navajo man, Luis Horseman, by a Navajo wolf, a witch in the local lore. The story introduces the middle-aged Navajo Tribal Police lieutenant Joe Leaphorn, a man of immense patience who "disliked illogic in others and detested it in himself." Leaphorn is a pragmatist with a master's degree in anthropology from Arizona State, a man of science who firmly believes in an orderly universe. The real hero of *The Blessing Way*, however, turns out to be an anthropologist named Bergen McKee rather than Leaphorn.

It was not until his second Navajo novel in 1973, *Dance Hall of the Dead*, that Hillerman seemed to understand that Leaphorn, the partially assimilated Indian, was his hero, a man caught between two worlds, working hard to exist in both and destroy neither. But even in *The Blessing Way* Hillerman intuited the source of strength in his work. First, the land: "The foothills of the Lukachukais shimmered under the blinding sun— gray mesquite and creosote bush, gray-green scrub cedar, and the paler gray of the eroded gullies; and above the grayness the blue-green of the higher slopes shaded now by an embryo early-afternoon thundercloud." The land was more than a backdrop for the mystery—it was a primary player in the action, filled with beauty and hazard, a landscape of ancient ruins and treasures, talus slopes and cliff houses, eroded sandstone figures and eerie silences. The setting both stimulated conflict and consumed it. Also, Navajo religion and culture were threaded perfectly into the story line. Here, in *The Blessing Way*, Leaphorn talks about evil: "When the water rose in the Fourth World and the Holy People emerged through the hollow reed, First Man and First Woman came up, too. But they forgot witchcraft and so they sent Diving Heron back for it. They told him to bring out 'the way to get rich' so the Holy People wouldn't know what he was getting. And Heron brought it out and gave it to First Man and First Woman and they gave some of it to Snake. But Snake couldn't swallow it so he had to hold it in his mouth. And that's why it kills you when a snake strikes you." From talk of religion, it is natural to speak of culture, and later Leaphorn contemplates why Navajos kill: "Not as lightly as white men, because the Navajo Way made life the ultimate value and death unrelieved terror. Usually the motive for homicide on the Reservation was simple. Anger, or fear, or a mixture of both. Or a mixture of one with alcohol. Navajos didn't kill with cold-blooded premeditation. Nor did they kill for profit. To do so violated the scale of values of The People. Beyond meeting simple immediate needs, the Navajo Way placed little worth on property. In fact, being richer than one's clansmen carried with it a social stigma. It was unnatural, and therefore suspicious." The Navajo tradition is one that honors unselfishness and sharing above private gain. Most Navajos, as Leaphorn suggests, have not acquired enough of white culture to murder for gain.

"In Leaphorn," Hillerman writes in *Listening Woman* (1978), "the Navajo sensitivity to land and landscape was fine tuned." Leaphorn is a man who has trained in the white man's world and been nurtured in the Navajo Way, and therefore seems a perfect lens through which to observe Navajo life, especially in its clashes with the dominant white culture. But, perhaps, with *People of Darkness* (1980) Hillerman found an even more striking medium for his message in the person of Jim Chee. Chee, a Tribal officer in his early thirties, has studied anthropology and American literature at the University of New Mexico, and he is also studying to be a *yataalii*, a medicine man or singer of the sacred Navajo ceremonies. Like Leaphorn, Chee has a deeply embedded "Navajo sense of balance, order, and harmony." But studying to be a shaman while being a police officer was "like being an investment banker and a Catholic priest at the same time." It's the odd tension between these two vocations, holy man and man of the law, that gives Chee such a pointed perspective. Although both men have profound feelings for their world and their people's way of life, Chee is unlike Leaphorn in many ways. Where Leaphorn is a pragmatist, Chee is a dreamer. He believes in the power of witchcraft; Leaphorn believes only in its effects. One is a romantic, the other a skeptic. Chee, imaginative and intuitive, has a poetic nature; Leaphorn, realistic and rational, has a scientific one. The older man goes through channels, while the younger is a free spirit, but both finally are seeking harmony, looking for the transcendent pattern in their world, be it spiritual or scientific.

After *The Dark Wind* (1982) and *The Ghostway* (1984), Hillerman brought the two police officers together in *Skinwalkers* (1988), a union he has maintained through his last four books. Bringing the two characters together has been like setting two halves of human nature in relief against one another. In Chee and Leaphorn, we see youth and age or the separate and distinct inclinations toward metaphor and fact. Hillerman dramatizes both the chasm between the two and the bridge that connects them. In *Skinwalkers*, although Leaphorn initially suspects his young colleague of being involved with criminals, they manage to form a grudging alliance. Perhaps not a match made in heaven, it works on the reservation despite their differences, which extend even to their physical characteristics. Chee has a "longish, narrow face fitting a longish, narrow body—all shoulders and no hips. The 'Tuba City Navajo,' as some anthropologists had labeled the type. Pure Athabascan genetics. Tall, long torso, narrow pelvis, destined to be a skinny old man. Leaphorn himself fell into the 'Checkerboard type.' He represented—according to this authority—a blood/gene mix with the Pueblo peoples. Leaphorn didn't particularly like the theory, but it was useful ammunition when Emma pressed him to get his weight and belt size down a bit." Leaphorn is a legend and Chee something of an upstart. Leaphorn "had no tolerance for witchcraft or anything about it—for those who believed in witches, or stories about skinwalkers, corpse sickness, the cures for same, and everything connected with the Navajo Wolves." On the other hand, "Like a nonfundamentalist Christian, Chee believed in the poetic metaphor of the Navajo story of human genesis." They are separated—Chee stationed on the northern edge of the reservation in Shiprock and Leaphorn in the south in Window Rock—by more than just miles.

Despite their differences, though, they are both Navajos, and both men who believe in and seek a transcendent order. Scientist or shaman, each is rooted in Navajo spirituality, touched by the very sacredness of the land given to them by the gods. As men and detectives they search ultimately for meaning. In the last three novels—*A Thief of Time* (1988), *Talking God* (1989), and *Coyote Waits* (1990)—the two men come closer together. In *A Thief of Time* they are joined by a kinship of loneliness. Leaphorn's wife, Emma, has died, and Chee's girlfriend, Mary Landon, has returned to the Midwest. A famous anthropologist vanishes, and the detectives' separate paths converge as the lines of the

New Mexico/Arizona

crimes they are attempting to solve become entwined. Their world views are still very different. Leaphorn has decided that Chee is a romantic, "a man who followed dreams. The sort who would have joined that Paiute shaman who invented the ghost dance and the vision of white men withering away and the buffalo coming back to the plains. Maybe that wasn't fair. It was more that Chee seemed to think an island of 180,000 Navajos could live the old way in a white ocean. Perhaps 20,000 of them could, if they were happy on mutton, cactus, and piñon nuts. Not practical. Navajos had to compete in the real world. The Navajo Way didn't teach competition. Far from it." But even though they are philosophically at odds, the two come close together at the conclusion of the story when Leaphorn asks Chee to perform a sing for him.

In the most recent story, *Coyote Waits*, Leaphorn and Chee have come to bear a strong resemblance to one another, like a father and son who after years of conflict recognize how much they are alike, more than they have ever been willing to admit. In the final pages the narrator says, "Leaphorn considered Officer Jim Chee. A screwup, but an interesting young man. Intelligent, the way he had made the connections to tie everything in. But he'd never make a good administrator. Never. Nor a team player, and law enforcement often required that. Maybe he would work better in criminal investigations. Like Leaphorn."

Coyote Waits ends on a note of rebirth for symbolic

father and son. Leaphorn, who will always mourn the loss of his wife, has returned fully to the world and to his job. He has even asked Professor Louisa Bourebonette if she would go to China with him where he wants to look into his Athabascan origins in Mongolia. Janet Pete, Chee's Navajo lawyer-friend, is returning to the reservation, to the Navajo world, and to Chee. In the final analysis, perhaps this, not murder, is what all of Hillerman's books are about.

His stories center upon the search for *hozro*, and the conflict between the Navajo Way and the white man's way. Jim Chee and Joe Leaphorn, representatives of the Navajo path, know how to love and seek beauty in their lives. More often than not, the white world is peopled with cold killers whose twisted understanding of love is chilling. Colton Wolf, with eyes that were faint blue-green, "about the tint of old ice," has a look that is "bleached, drained of pigment, antiseptic, neat, emotionless," as cold a killer and as frightening an example of modern man as any to be encountered in recent fiction. Like Colton Wolf, Leroy Fleck of *Talking God* is a cold-blooded killer with a mother fixation. Vaggan, the hired killer in *The Ghostway*, is an image out of *The Godfather*, a coolly efficient murderer who calmly decapitates Dobermans, fills bags with blood, and clamps cattle tags through the ears of a talk-show host who doesn't pay his gambling debts. But Hillerman's villains are also human beings, so much so that Timothy Foote in the *New York Times Book Review* described Leroy

Fleck as a "curiously winsome Dickensian character, an urban hit man who knifes his victims with surgical skill but spends his off-duty hours trying desperately to find a nursing home willing to keep his savagely obstreperous mother."

The anthropologists that Hillerman depicts are typically not much more admirable representatives of the white world than the Vaggans or the Flecks. Most often they are greedy or ambitious. "Publish or perish" is more than a metaphor for Hillerman's academics. In a recent interview he was asked, "It's only a joke that they'd kill to publish. Right?" Hillerman replied, "I'm not so sure." His academics are often proud status seekers. Professors Tagert of *Coyote Waits* and Reynolds of *Dance Hall of the Dead*, or the graduate student Ted Isaacs and the young engineer Jim Hall, trade love for power and fame, human intimacy for a place in the world. Even the predominantly white FBI in Hillerman's novels is at best incompetent, at worst corrupt.

The worst sins in Hillerman's universe are greed and brutal ambition. When these white motives enter the reservation they sweep in like an evil wind, and crimes in this world can only be solved by someone, a Jim Chee or a Joe Leaphorn, who understands the land and the people, and the shapes that evil can assume under the hard, empty blue sky, the luxurious clouds, and among the shadow and light of the deserts, mesas, and mountains. In striving to find order in the chaos created by evil, Leaphorn and Chee must be connected to the geography of their people, both literal and spiritual. The balance they discover results in justice, if not always legal correctness, for both detectives are more concerned with harmony in the universe than with the law. Like Sam Spade or Philip Marlowe, they bend the rules in order to achieve justice.

Hillerman's achievement in his Navajo novels is a considerable one. Michael Parfit, in *Smithsonian*, said, "The form of expression he has chosen is stranger than sorcery here, but within his spare prose Hillerman has caught the nature of both the land and its people so richly that the Navajos have honored him as a 'special friend to the *Dineh*.'" And Michael Dorris wrote in the *New York Times Book Review* that "Hillerman's picture of modern American Indians is never patronizing, never hokey, never precious." Readers finish his books, as Dorris mentions, "with the impression of having visited, vividly though briefly, a place and a people unlike any other. That a mystery is astutely solved as well seems almost a bonus."

> *More than half of the continent's uranium and much of its petroleum and coal lies beneath Indian land, and so the Indians are in the way again.*
>
> —Peter Matthiessen,
> *In the Spirit of Crazy Horse*

New Mexico/Arizona

The mystery that Hillerman probes over and over again in his novels is a cultural and historical one. The backdrop to all of his work is the story of the Navajos, a story that is shrouded in some uncertainty. *Navajo* is a Spanish word usually interpreted as "the place of the great planted fields," though some historians suggest that the meaning is "a worthless, flat piece of land." In their own tongue, the Navajos are *Dineh*, "The People." Linguistic cousins to the Apaches, the Navajos are part of the Athabascan people who journeyed from Asia over a land bridge in the Bering Strait more than thirteen thousand years ago. One seventeenth-century friar spoke of the Navajos as "the Apaches of the planted fields." The Navajos, like the Apaches, emigrated from Alaska and northwestern Canada around the tenth century looking for a new homeland to the south. They settled in the Southwest some time between the eleventh and the sixteenth centuries, most scientists and historians say, but the area had been occupied for a long time before they arrived.

As early as 10,000 B.C. the beginnings of a desert culture sprouted in the present American Southwest. Archaeologists believe that by 100 B.C. the Anasazi (which in Navajo means "ancient ones") had established prehistoric settlements. The Anasazi, the first known civilized American Indian culture, were basket makers and weavers who lived in caves or in shelters made of adobe. Originally hunters and gatherers, the Anasazi eventually moved toward agriculture and pottery. By 700 A.D. the

Pueblo culture, descendants of the Anasazi, developed multistoried, terraced cliff dwellings. In these apartment buildings carved into the sides of mountains, the Pueblos perfected their pottery and weaving.

When the Navajos arrived from the northwest, they encountered the Pueblos and soon after the Spanish conquistadors who had begun exploring the New World. By the early sixteenth century the conquests of Cortez and Pizarro sharpened the lust for riches and stimulated the search for gold into the northern Indian culture. Instead of gold, however, Coronado and his followers discovered only a primitive people eking out a bare existence in an uninviting environment. Nevertheless, by 1598 the Spanish began establishing settlements in Arizona and New Mexico, bringing to a head the conflict between Navajos and Spaniards. Both groups raided, the Navajos for stock, the Spanish for slaves. Temporary peace treaties were negotiated intermittently, allowing herding and farming to become more rewarding than raiding, but in 1680 the Pueblos, most likely assisted by the Navajos and Apaches, successfully rebelled against Spanish dominion, driving settlers, soldiers, and missionaries out of New Mexico.

But this story was written primarily in the blood of Native Americans and was virtually the same for every tribe on the continent. It took eighty years of horror and violence to bring about the explosive expulsion of the Spanish. The Spanish rule was a reign of terror described by Willa Cather in *Death Comes for the Arch-*

bishop: "In those days, before the American occupation, 'hunting Navajos' needed no pretext, it was a form of sport. A company of Mexicans would ride west to Navajo country, raid a few sheep camps, and come home bringing flocks of ponies and a bunch of prisoners, for every one of whom they received a large bounty from the Mexican government." Only a little more than a decade after their expulsion, however, the Spanish returned, even stronger. By 1692 the Spaniards were already coming back, and within four years they were in full control again. The relationship between Navajos and Spaniards did not get any better on the second try. By the nineteenth century they were waging almost constant warfare against one another. Navajo and Apache raiders took nearly a half-million sheep from Spanish–American settlements in one period alone in midcentury. As Raymond Friday Locke makes clear in *The Book of the Navajo*, "Navajo history of the period between the defeat of the Pueblos and the conquest of New Mexico by the United States in 1846 consists of little more than a long list of raids and counter-raids, of expeditions and punitive expeditions."

In 1821, when Spain gave up all its American mainland possessions and New Mexico became a province of Mexico, many merchants and trappers came to Santa Fe and Taos. In 1846 President Polk declared war on Mexico and in the same year General Kearny and the United States Army of the West took Santa Fe without firing a shot. On August 18, 1846, New Mexico became part of the United States. At first the Navajos may have believed that the Americans, enemies of the Mexicans, were logically their allies. But soon this illusion disappeared, and they realized that the American victory meant only more settlers, more death, and an even more concerted attempt at the destruction of their culture. This is the beginning of what historians call the American period for the Navajos, a time, as Clyde Kluckhorn and Dorothea Leighton say, of "numerous military operations, of the establishment of army posts within Navajo territory, of the arrival of the first civilian agents to the Navajos, of a succession of Navajo raids and 'incidents,' of unsuccessful attempts to bring peace and stability by negotiation." This was the high point of the American philosophy of Manifest Destiny, articulated by John O'Sullivan in *United States Magazine and Democratic Review* in the summer of 1845. "It is our manifest destiny," he intoned, "to overspread the continent allotted by Providence for the free development of our yearly multiplying millions." In the arithmetic of America's Manifest Destiny it was easiest not to count Native Americans as human beings. The "New Men," as the Navajo Chief Narbona called the American soldiers, were different from the Spaniards only in their complexion.

In 1863 the United States government attempted to erase the "Navajo problem." Under the direction of General James H. Carleton, Colonel Kit Carson and seven hundred New Mexico volunteers invaded Navajo lands. Carleton's plan was simple: hunt down and kill or capture all Navajos until they surrendered and agreed to live on a single reservation where they could be transformed into "good Christians." Carleton wanted *Dinehtah*, the land of the Navajos, because he was convinced that it contained a wealth of mineral riches. By 1864 the war was over. More than three hundred Navajos had been killed in battle, and an uncounted number had been starved to death, killed by civilians, and sold into slavery. Like most other Native Americans in the nineteenth century, the Navajos were viewed by most of white America as either savages or untutored children. In essence, the government decided, the Navajos needed to be controlled or exterminated. General Carleton's command to Kit Carson had been to embark on a "scorched-earth" policy, to enslave the Navajos by destroying their homeland. Even Willa Cather, who virtually canonized Carson in *Death Comes for the Archbishop*, said that he did a soldier's brutal work in an act of misguided loyalty.

The major Navajo stronghold was Canyon de Chelly, which cut thirty miles west from the Chuska Mountains. The red rock walls of Canyon de Chelly, which rise to one thousand feet in some places and are as close as fifty yards apart in others, have overhanging ledges that made superb defensive positions. Within this sanctuary, the Navajos raised corn, wheat, and fruit, or grazed sheep and goats. The Navajos were especially proud of the peach orchards that they had tended since the days of Spanish domination. Under orders from General Carleton, Carson and his men moved into Fort Defiance at the mouth of the canyon and began forays into the Navajo stronghold, bringing out livestock and harvesting or destroying all the corn and wheat they could find. Perhaps the most psychologically devastating act for the Navajos was the destruction of their peach orchards. Carson and his men laid waste to the land, destroying food caches, taking sheep and cattle, and burning hogans, wheat fields, and more than five thousand peach trees. This destruction broke the spirit of the Navajo people.

With their food supply gone, they were reduced to eating piñon nuts. Starving and freezing to death, most Navajos surrendered and were sent on a long march to Fort Sumner and the Bosque Redondo down on the Pecos, away from the land of their people. Bosque Redondo, a strip of land 175 miles southwest of Santa Fe, was near the alkaline waters of the Rio Pecos and, as Raymond Friday Locke says, "a few ragged stands of cottonwoods." It didn't matter that it was open to all the elements, unattractive, and difficult to farm. For Carleton it was the ideal location to place the people he referred to as "those wolves of the mountains." At the Bosque Redondo, herded into adobe-walled compounds, they were treated like prisoners of war, despite General Carleton's unctuous words of paternalism. According to Dee Brown in *Bury My Heart at Wounded Knee*, "They lived like prairie dogs in burrows. . . .

Crowded together as they were, disease began to take a toll of the weaker ones." Many tried to escape, to return to their homeland.

Some writers have compared the Navajo experience at Bosque Redondo to the southerners' experience in the Civil War and its lingering effects. In ways, though, it was more like a concentration camp experience, one that came close to extinguishing even a flickering hope in the hearts of The People. But photographs of the Navajo warriors at Bosque Redondo show the proud high-cheekboned Asian contours, the defiantly clenched jaws, and the fiery, hypnotic eyes looking toward the land they were forced to leave behind.

It was on March 6, 1864, that the Navajos had begun their "Long Walk" south three hundred miles from their homeland to Fort Sumner. Some, however, never surrendered, vanishing into the Grand Canyon or seeking asylum with rebellious bands of Apaches. The Navajo leader Manuelito steadfastly refused to give up. He remained in the mountains for two more years with about one hundred men, women, and children, saying, "It is a tradition of my people that we must never cross the three rivers—the Grande, the San Juan, the Colorado. Nor could I leave the Chuska Mountains. I was born there. I shall remain. I have nothing to lose but my life, and that they can come and take whenever they please, but I will not move." But in September 1866 Manuelito, emaciated and wounded, his people sick and dying and with no arrows left for their bows, surrendered.

THE PRESENT

By 1868, though, even the usually purblind United States government had to admit that it had made a terrible mistake at Bosque Redondo. It had been four years of disease, poverty, and misery for the Navajos. On the morning of June 18, 1868, the Navajos began their long walk back to the reservation in Arizona and New Mexico in a column that stretched across the desert for ten miles. Despite the fact that they returned to a wasteland—fields covered with weeds, orchards in charred ruins, livestock gone—many of them knelt and wept when they came within sight of Mount Taylor, outside of Albuquerque. They survived by scratching out an existence hunting and gathering. They endured, perhaps even thrived, in their cherished landscape. By 1892 the Navajo population had more than doubled to eighteen thousand.

On their land, amidst their four holy mountains, the Navajos, according to Garrick Bailey, "remained as they had always been—a population separated from the rest of American society by a strong sense of tribal identity." Traditional Navajos believe that their ancestors came out of the earth, led up through a series of subterranean worlds to the surface by Holy People. This is the core of the Navajo experience: they came from the earth and they are inextricably connected to it. Today the Navajo Nation is the largest Indian tribe in the United States. Despite a history of broken promises, a flooding tide of white immigrants, violence and prejudice, the Navajos have endured, holding fast in large part to their beliefs, customs, and their sacred homeland, a landscape described by Edward Abbey as "naked, monolithic, austere and unadorned as the sculpture of the moon . . . a desert place, clean, pure, totally useless and unprofitable."

> *It was Hosteen Nakai who had chosen Jimmy*
> *Chee's "war name," which was Long Thinker.*
> *Thus his uncle was one of the very few who*
> *knew his real and secret identity.*
> —Tony Hillerman, *People of Darkness*

Just as I had first encountered the South through the fiction of Walker Percy, I first saw the Southwest of the Navajos through the stories of Tony Hillerman. His books drew me toward the place and the people, like a light shining through a half-opened door.

I flew into Albuquerque, rented a car, and headed toward Window Rock, Arizona, the capital of the Navajo Nation and, like the sandstone formation that gives the town its name, an opening into the separate world of the reservation. I drove west on Route 40, past the Sandia Mountains and Mount Taylor, a three-hour drive during which Michael Dorris's words from *The Broken Cord* echoed in my mind: "No two reservations are alike any more than any two tribes are the same, but there are commonalities: government housing, missionaries, powwows, internal political feuds, disproportionate representation within the population of the very old and the very young, ironic twists of humor, raging debates about alcohol, the Bureau of Indian Affairs, broken cars, quiet. People know each other, know who's who and who's related to whom. That counts for plenty and extends an umbrella of tolerance, acceptance, and non-criticism rarely offered in mainstream communities. If you belong, you belong. If you're a stranger, you feel it like a constant prickle of electricity." As I drove toward Window Rock, Joe Leaphorn territory, I tuned the radio to 89.9 FM and heard something that I had never heard on a station back east but which seemed natural now: a Navajo chant, a chorus of voices, a tonal language that sounded Oriental, a language at once beautiful and distant and alien. For twenty minutes I listened to words that I didn't understand but that made sense to me— until the radio announcer came on the air and in the soft cadences of a Navajo said, "I'll see you whenever I come on air again. Thanks for listening. If you are traveling, go safely." Then silence, as if the station disappeared, as if sound had been sucked into the open spaces. I drove on, into "that great emptiness," listening, my neck prickling in anticipation as lightning lit the sky in front of me and the first huge drops of rain splattered against the windshield.

A few miles down the road and the sky was clear again. The world seems to come into clearer focus when the spaces are so wide open. All around me there were miles and miles of beautiful desolation, deep blue skies and lush clouds. The high desert land along the highway seemed various—yellow, gold, purple and brown—with rabbit brush, snake weed, tumbleweed, and an occasional cluster of stunted junipers. For miles on end there was nothing that my city eyes were used to, no cars or buildings or people. Instead there were red rock buttes, windmills and water tanks, and once a train that snaked out through the flattened miles to the south. As I watched it, time seemed to have little meaning in these distances. It could have been 1902 as readily as 1992.

The mountains far to the south turned purple in the dusk, and the adobe-walled hogans sank more deeply into the colors around them. In *Death Comes for the Archbishop* Willa Cather said that it had always been the white man's way to assert dominion in any landscape, to change it and make it over to fit his personality, but "it was the Indian's way to pass through a country without disturbing anything; to pass and leave no trace, like fish through water, or birds through air. . . . It was the Indian manner to vanish into the landscape, not to stand out against it. . . . The Navajo hogans, among the sand and willows, were made of sand and willows."

The next morning I parked my rental car in the shadow of the Window Rock monument, near Tribal Police headquarters. From eight to nine I waited in the receptionist's area, as acid rock played from a radio on her desk and an old man with one crutch and a battered cowboy hat hobbled around the room smiling at everyone. Sgt. Whitegoat was in a meeting. Every few seconds, laughter erupted from behind the closed door. There seemed to be no rush. We were on Navajo time, and I whiled it away imagining the lives of the officers listed on the roster board: Etsitty, Yellowhorse, Yazzie, Begay. It could have been a list of minor characters in Hillerman's novels. In one instant the past and present seemed to blur and cross each other as a weathered old woman hidden in shawls and skirts, an image from Bosque Redondo, passed a handsome young officer who was flirting with one of the secretaries.

When Wally Whitegoat emerged from the meeting, he glanced in my direction and shook my hand Navajo style, lightly, hands barely touching. A fraction over six feet tall, Whitegoat is half a foot taller than the average Navajo. He has been a Tribal Police officer for twelve of his thirty years. For his first three years on the job he was too young to buy his own bullets legally, so his parents had to buy them for him. Perhaps with that in mind, he now makes his own ammunition.

Before Whitegoat and I could sit down to talk, he had to drive a Navajo woman home. Her husband had threatened her. I rode in the back of the Chevy Blazer, behind the prisoner's gate, until we got to her house, made sure everything was peaceful and the husband was not around, and returned to the open road.

Approximately 300 officers make up the Tribal force, and they cover the 25,000 square miles of the reservation. In Virginia Beach, where I live, 599 officers patrol 259 square miles. In Virginia Beach, of course, 400,000 people are squeezed into that space. Less than half that number lives on the reservation on 100 times the amount of land. The 30 officers in Window Rock, a town of about 5,000, cover 150 square miles on an average day. Unlike the Hopis, who gather together in towns, Navajos scatter across the countryside. Families cluster together like junipers on the open range, sometimes miles of dirt roads between one group and another. As one character in *Skinwalkers* says, "Nobody gets out here except on purpose."

Driving across these great spaces can be tiring, 250 miles between one station and another, but Whitegoat, like the protagonists of Hillerman's books, finds great pleasure in what that openness bestows. Like Jim Chee in *Coyote Waits* he will stop occasionally to view a sunset: "North, over Sleeping Ute Mountain in Colorado, over Utah's Abajo Mountains, great thunderheads were reaching toward their evening climax. Their tops, reflecting in the direct sun, were snowy white and the long streamers of ice crystals blown from them seemed to glitter. But at lower levels the light that struck them had been filtered through the clouds over the Chuskas and turned into shades of rose, pink, and red. Lower still, the failing light mottled them from pale blue-gray to the deepest blue. Overhead, the streaks of high level cirrus clouds were being ignited by the sunset. They drove through a fiery twilight."

Like Chee and most Navajos, Whitegoat feels a spiritual connection to the land. Raymond Friday Locke says that there is no such thing as religion in the usual sense in Navajo culture because everything is religious. "Everything a Navajo knows," says Locke, "his shelter, his fields, his livestock, the sky above him and the ground upon which he walks—is holy." Whitegoat lives in a log hogan on his family's 130-acre homesite. The hogan, a six-sided dwelling with the doorway facing east and a smoke hole in the center, is the traditional Navajo dwelling, and although most families no longer live in hogans, a majority still build one on their property. Native ceremonies can be conducted only in a hogan. Even though last month he had a traditional sing in his hogan to bring health and success to himself and his family, Whitegoat's hogan seemed to straddle two worlds. The building itself cost less than five hundred dollars to build about ten years ago. It is as simple and utilitarian as any Navajo home on the outside, but inside it is cluttered with things from the white world—a hotplate, microwave oven, tables, chairs, a stereo television, a VCR. Next month he will move his wife and two young children, who have been living for the past few months at her parents' house, into a place in town. When he does this, he will retrieve his satellite dish from a friend's house and hook it up.

As he leaned against the polished drawers of a new bureau that supported a tank containing his seven-year-old goldfish, his "only pet," he played with the predator calls he had made out of pen tops. The sounds he made were bloodcurdling and lifelike—a screeching cottontail, a squawking bird, a dying prairie dog—sounds that would draw coyotes toward him as he stood on the edge of some clearing with one of the thirty rifles he had collected over the years. He hunted coyotes most avidly in the winter when their pelts were full, and once when pelts were averaging twenty dollars apiece, he got twelve in a single day.

On our way towards his family's ten-acre planting ground, we passed the homemade corral that houses Animal, the horse he recently bought for $150. Originally called Thunder, the horse had not yet lived up to its name, and Whitegoat acknowledged it with mocking good humor and a handful of feed. His sense of humor, like that of most Navajos, and perhaps appropriately for such a country, is dry. His own warrior name is so secret, he said, "I don't even know it any more. I forget what it was, the name my uncle gave me."

When we reached the field of corn, he pointed out the movement of prairie dogs through the paths between the stalks. "Tonight I'll get that one," he said and looked back toward the hogan and other houses on the ridge of the hill, wishing, it seemed, that he had time to go back for a rifle. He pointed to the doors of the small frame buildings and said, "You don't need a compass on the reservation. Look for the door on any house—then you'll know the east."

On the far side of the corn field was a wash that we crossed to get to the charred remains of his family's old hogan, burnt down long before Whitegoat was born because a family member died in it. Whitegoat told me to be careful where I stepped with my tennis shoes, and to keep an eye out for snakes, but as we stood near the circle of burnt wood lying on the dirt—an outline of the hogan that was once there—I sensed other dangers, too.

Traditional Navajos have no belief in a Christian sort of afterlife, but they do believe in the negative effects of a *chindi*, the spirit of the dead. Death and everything associated with it are repulsive to the traditional Navajos, and the dead are buried with haste. A *chindi* hogan, a house in which a person dies, is either abandoned or burned to the ground. Joe Leaphorn in *Dance Hall of the Dead* comes upon a home haunted in such a way: "Now the hogan was cold, hostile to him, occupied not by Shorty Bowlegs but by Shorty's ghost—a ghost which would in Navajo fashion embody only those things in his father's nature which were weak, evil, angry." The rational Leaphorn enters the hogan to investigate, but he does so reluctantly. In *The Ghostway*, however, the more traditional Jim Chee responds differently: "It was through the north wall of a hogan that a corpse must be removed in the sad event of death striking someone inside. Then the smoke hole would be plugged, the entrance boarded, and the place abandoned—with the corpse hole left open to warn the People that this had become a death hogan. The body could be removed, but never the malicious *chindi* of the dead person. The ghost infection was permanent." Chee circles around the place, but lets the *belagana*, the white man, enter the hogan to search.

Like Leaphorn, Whitegoat seemed able to step past such ideas. He crossed the invisible line where the walls once stood and walked into the center of the hogan. Inside that circle we talked of my home as well as his. His long-jawed Navajo face looked down as I spoke. He waited after I stopped talking, letting the silence stretch out toward the distant rumble of a jet in the eastern sky. The white man's custom of expecting a listener to do more than listen, to sigh and murmur, smile and gasp, was not the Navajo manner. Where perhaps it is courtesy in the white world to swat silence away like an intruding bug, it is Navajo courtesy to wait, to be certain the speaker has finished. Where one culture demands eye contact, the other sees it as rudeness. But our language was the same, even if our cadences and culture were different, and with the ashes of his ancestors at our feet and the rolling hills of his family compound before us, we spoke of our childhoods and dreams.

"I've always wanted to be a police officer," he said. "Manuelito, a great hero of our people, was the first Tribal officer." With that, he took off his sunglasses and touched the stem against his badge—"Protect and Serve—1868." "Manuelito was the first," he said again. "All my dreams have always been here—in Dinehtah. I've seen films about New York and other big places, people jammed together like sheep in a pen. This is where I want to be. White people are run by clocks. I run on Indian time, and I live in the Navajo Nation. The reason why the government gave it back to us was because they thought it was a wasteland. That nobody could do anything with it. But this is our sacred ground, and I can't imagine being anywhere else. There are no mansions out here. Only small frame houses. Basic, simple. No chandeliers or fancy-scented toilet paper—how's that going to help you? We're all connected out here, to our ancestors, our family, the land. And even though I'm not traditional, I believe in our way, in prayer, in the power of sings." Recalling the sing that was performed for him last month, he said, "The medicine man might sound like a baby if you heard him talking in English, but in Navajo he is a philosopher, a wise man whose words are like magic."

We stepped from that invisible circle and crossed to another hill, plucking two cones from a piñon tree along the way and peeling the sticky sap-filled bark with our teeth until we came to the smoky tasting nut inside. The hill we stood on was an Anasazi site, dotted with yucca plants, arrowheads, and shards of pottery. Here I felt as if I were in a scene from a Hillerman story, with history all around me and Whitegoat, like Jim Chee, standing next to me but positioned between the white world and his own. There, amid the cactus plants and goat tracks, he talked of a novel he often thought of writing. He had been thinking of it for years. "It's the story of a Tribal Police officer who sees a plane crash on the reservation and goes to investigate. He is knocked out by drug traffickers and taken across the border into Mexico. Eventually he escapes and uses his survival skills to make the long walk through the wilderness back into Arizona. I plan to go into detail about how to cook a rabbit, find edible plants, look for water in the desert, call in game. During that long two-week walk home, the officer thinks about his wife and two kids. He is about to get a divorce and he begins to see he is making the wrong decision."

I didn't have to be a Navajo tracker to see where the story started or where it led. As we drove back to Window Rock in the Tribal Police carryall, I saw that fiction and fact often grow together and that Wally Whitegoat was happy, a man who walked in beauty.

> *Shiprock stuck up like a blue thumb on the western horizon. . . .*
>
> —Tony Hillerman, *A Thief of Time*

When I saw Shiprock floating like a ghost vessel on the desert air, its sandstone sails luffed out in breezes from the archaeological past, I knew I had entered Jim Chee's home ground. Near the Shiprock police station the San Juan River flowed through groves of cottonwoods and past scores of trailers, any of which could have fit the description of Chee's place, private and isolated.

THE PRESENT

At the Tribal Police station in town, Thomas T. Horse, a medicine man in the Peyote Church and a Tribal officer as well, directed me toward the youth center, the only structure besides the Shiprock monument that stood out from the homogeneous squalor of the government housing that seemed to blanket the town. As Horse left on his assignment, I headed toward the domed center in the middle of what had once been the largest town on the reservation.

Eighteen-year-old Orson Hobson, who had just graduated from Shiprock High School, and wanted, eventually, like Jim Chee, to go to college, maybe the University of New Mexico, was shooting baskets when I entered the gym. We played a game of Twenty-One. He made his first three shots, but I made the next sixteen in a row and the game was over. Orson had been the starting pointing guard on his high school team, but he was only five-feet-six and too amiable to be very aggressive against a stranger, I think.

When we hopped up on the bleachers to talk, he took off his UNLV hat and waved to his fifteen-year-old sister Pamela who sat across the gymnasium from us. He was certain that basketball is the most important sport on the reservation, although when I told him that an older Navajo man had said to me that "The four most important sports on the reservation are rodeo, rodeo, rodeo, and basketball," he smiled in agreement. Our conversation drifted from the state championship in track and field that Shiprock had won the previous year to Orson's recent reading of *Listening Woman*. Although he was not taught the traditional beliefs growing up in the nonprofit housing that edges this border town, he said that many of his friends believe in witches. "Some of them have seen them." But he did not say much more, perhaps revealing himself to be more traditional than he realizes, for it is considered unwise to speak too much of witches because they are capable of causing illness or death. Like ghosts, they go about at night dressed in the skins of wolves or coyotes, doing harm to those they dislike.

In some ways Orson is probably a typical young man living in such a border town on the reservation. He can't find a job; there simply are not enough to go around. He sees his father, who works as a custodian in Flagstaff, only occasionally. His mother is a maid for a local doctor. He has dreams—to study hotel management—but there are no hotels or motels in Shiprock (although in flush times there were two), so he will have to live out his dreams elsewhere. At one time Shiprock had high hopes for itself. In the 1960s there was a promising irrigation project, but by the mid-1970s the project failed, as Ray Begaye, the executive director of the youth center, said, "because the money dried up and the leadership collapsed."

Without one of the branches of Navajo Community College in Shiprock, the town might literally become filled with ghosts. But the picture is not much different on the reservation even outside border towns like Ship-rock. According to the Navajo Nation Bureau of Economic Development, the per capita income on the reservation in 1991 was $5,958 in a country where the average income is over $19,000. Nearly half of all the people who reside on the reservation live in poverty. About two out of five finish high school and fewer than one out of twenty goes on to graduate from college. In 1968 in *Desert Solitaire* Edward Abbey wrote: "They [the Navajos] are the Negroes of the Southwest—red black men. Like their cousins in the big cities they turn for solace, quite naturally, to alcohol and drugs. . . . The Navajos sink even deeper into . . . squalor, unemployment or irregular and ill-paid employment, broken families, disease, prostitution, crime, alcoholism, lack of education, too many children, apathy and demoralization and various forms of mental illness, including evangelical Protestantism."

But it's places like the Shiprock Youth Center and the Navajo Community College and people like the thirty-five-year-old Ray Begaye who are determined to try to make changes without destroying the culture. When Begaye received his master's degree in public administration from Arizona State, he had two job offers immediately, one to be a principal in Cortez and another to be a community coordinator in a large city; both paid over forty thousand dollars, but he took the job in Ship-rock, which pays twenty-five thousand dollars, because he grew up here and he wanted to come back to help. He had been a gang member in his youth, but with some help he had managed to change the direction of his life. He wanted to return the favor.

He remembered riding through Gallup with his father when he was a boy. "I can still see those old men, or they seemed old to me, passed out in the alleyways in the cold. I remember thinking then that when they are gone this will all be different. We will have learned. We will be too smart for alcohol. But now it's the younger ones out there."

On most reservations, alcohol abuse may be the most pressing social problem. According to *The Final Report of the American Indian Policy Review Commission* a few years ago, alcoholism and its effects are "the most severe and widespread health problem among Indians today." A 1975 study revealed that over 50 percent of all Native Americans who were surveyed had immediate family problems caused by drinking. In the 1960s, seven out of ten Indian arrests were alcohol-related. Fetal Alcohol Syndrome or Fetal Alcohol Effects touch the lives of one out of every four children on the reservations. FAS and FAE affect young people in a variety of ways, impairing them emotionally, intellectually, or physically. Michael Dorris in *The Broken Cord*, his powerful account of his adopted son's tragic battle with FAS, describes newborn babies whose skin smells of wine, as if they have been pickled in an amniotic sac filled with

Thunderbird or Ripple. He tells of undernourished babies who are thrown into delirium tremens when the cord is cut. He recounts stories of pregnant women on reservations drinking "Montana gin," Lysol mixed with water. Abusive drinking, as most experts suggest, is cyclical. Children of alcoholics are three times more likely to follow in the same path than children whose parents had no drinking problem.

"Places like the Shiprock Youth Center may break the insidious cycle," said Ray Begaye. "We get them hopefully before they begin drinking. If this center were not here, these kids would be out forming gangs." He paused, perhaps remembering his own past, and said, "I'm proud of the work we do with kids and hopeful it makes a difference."

Begaye is a small man. Glasses perch on his wide Navajo nose and scars are scratched into his upper lip like dry washes on the plateau outside. He was a black belt in karate but quit because he was accumulating too much scar tissue. "Grief can drive you places you never expected to go," he said, recalling a line in *The Broken Cord*, "but scars can teach you to be strong, that you can be healed."

When I left the youth center, Orson Hobson was still shooting baskets, driving to the right, spinning left and shooting a sweeping layup under the invisible outstretched arm of an imaginary opponent. He smiled shyly when he saw me and waved goodbye.

New Mexico/Arizona

. . . that mysterious and terrifying canyon.

—Willa Cather,
Death Comes for the Archbishop

My map of "Indian Country," produced by the Auto Club of Southern California, the same one tacked above Tony Hillerman's word processor and used by Joe Leaphorn and Jim Chee, was lying on the passenger's seat of my rental car as I pulled out of Window Rock a few days later. I had driven from Shiprock to Window Rock the day before, a long trip on Route 666, the kind of exhausting drive that Hillerman's officers do all the time. I cut across the backbone of the Chuska Mountains at Sheep Springs and followed Black Creek, past an occasional gas station and trading post, back to the Navajo Nation Inn. On the way back I saw far more sheep, cattle, and horses than people, and more goats than all four put together. Animals roamed the unfenced land and crossed the roads at will, and perhaps, as Emma Leaphorn said to her husband in *A Thief of Time*, the goat may be the perfect symbol for the *Dineh*: "It's starved, gaunt, bony, ugly. But look! It's tough. It endures."

I checked my map, wanting to follow the same route Hillerman does when he travels to Canyon de Chelly, going north on Navajo Route 12 along the west slope of the Chuskas, then circling back on Navajo 64 along the north rim. The sun had already lightened the sky at six o'clock when I started out, past the sandstone outcroppings to the east, still pink with the sun behind them. I got lost amid the boulders and dirt roads a few times and saw, even at that early hour, groups of Navajo children playing and women jogging along the side of the road. Storm clouds fell like streamers in the western sky.

I picked up a hitchhiker standing under a gnarled cypress tree. He was a Navajo man in about his mid-thirties; he looked wizened, withered by the dry climate and hard life. But his shy smile was strong. In halting English he amiably talked of his work as a roofer and pointed out the sights along the way—Wheatfields Lake, Crystal Wash, Red Lake. As we drove, I kept thinking about how different this country was from the eastern landscape I had come to know. In many ways this reservation seemed sad and impoverished, but the place and the people, in a strange way, reminded me of John McPhee's description of the Pine Barrens in New Jersey: "A visitor who stays awhile . . . soon feels that he is in another country, where attitudes and ambitions are at a variance with the American norm. People who drive around in the pines and see houses . . . with tar-paper peeling from the walls, and automobiles over-turned in the front yard, often decide, as they drive on, that they have just looked destitution in the face. I wouldn't call it that. I have yet to meet anyone living in the Pine Barrens who has in any way indicated envy of people who live elsewhere." It's difficult to imagine any two places that seem as radically different topographically as the Pine Barrens and the Navajo Reservation, but McPhee's description of "another country, where attitudes and ambition are at a variance with the American norm" aptly fits the Navajo land and people. I left the hitchhiker off at Tsaile and headed on 64 west into Chinle and the mouth of the canyon. He looked down politely when he said goodbye and in my rearview mirror I saw him wave. Like Wally Whitegoat, he seemed happy where he was, with little envy for those who lived in Phoenix or Tucson or anywhere else.

Shortly after I reached Chinle, I came upon what Hillerman had described in one of his books: "Seen from the rim, the canyon is awe-inspiring. Even the larger ruins seem too trivial to notice, overpowered by the vastness. But when you are on the surface below, the atmosphere is different. The cliffs close you into a very small place, with the outside world excluded. You exist in the bottom of a bottle. At locations such as Standing Cow Ruin, where reminders of man's efforts to survive and evolve surround you, this sense of human fragility and futility can be overwhelming."

I reached the visitor's center just a few minutes before a hike into the canyon was about to begin. Mine was the last name on the list of twenty for a four-hour expedition led by Ernestine Gray, a young Navajo woman who lives in the area. We descended a narrow and steep opening along a rocky path. "De Chelly" is a Spanish corruption of a Navajo word meaning "inside the rocks," and as we descended the temperature dropped, sounds changed timbre, and the present seemed far away. We stopped to examine the black streaks of canyon varnish, oxidation, along the sandstone walls; the juniper berries that Navajos associate with good health; and the bark that the Anasazis used to make their masks. We peered at the purple blossoms of Arizona thistle and the yellow buds of Snake Weed, gazed at the pictographs painted on the stone with ground gypsum and urine by a long-gone hand holding a pointed yucca leaf, and laughed at Ernestine's steady good humor.

Ernestine herself reminded me of a character in Hillerman's stories named Janet Pete, a small, skinny Navajo with short black hair, large black eyes, and a full share of confidence. Ernestine knew the canyon and her people. She knew herself, as well, it seemed. In general, women are a powerful presence in the Navajo culture. Every Navajo belongs to the clan of his mother, his "born to" group, but he is "born for" his father's clan. Wealth is passed down through the women. It came as no surprise that Ernestine could lead the twenty of us over the narrow rocky paths, across the open flats, through the dense foliage, and finally through the muddy waters of the flooded plain to the Anasazi site at First Ruins.

We sat around on the sandy canyon bottom, gazing up at the ancient dwellings or looking across the way at the tops of the scant cottonwoods that were rustling in the breeze. I daydreamed about Tony Hillerman's climbing down into Canyon de Chelly when he was working on his first book, *The Blessing Way*, paddling around on its quicksandy bottom and collecting a "headful of sensory impressions (the way the wind sounds down there, the nature of echoes, the smell of sage and wet sand, how the sky looks atop a tunnel of stone, the booming thunder bouncing from one cliff to another)." As Hillerman suggested, a hike into such a place stirs the imagination.

Forty families now live in the canyon, farming or sheepherding. In the winter they move to hogans somewhere along the rim. Once there were many more families. Once they thought this place impenetrable, perhaps the place where their people emerged from the lower worlds into the light. It was easy to imagine them here, those strong, defiant faces watching the Spanish, then the Americans, ruthlessly marching onto their holy ground. But the Navajos are still here, and it's still silent, breathtakingly beautiful. On our way out we passed a lone peach tree, planted long after Carson's fiery raid upon the Navajo orchards, and this small tree seemed as powerful a monument to the spirit of the people as any statue they could ever build.

And take upon's the mystery of things . . .
—Shakespeare, *King Lear*

It is a landscape in which secrets appear to drift in and out of focus in the waves of heat that flutter up from the

THE PRESENT

desert. In all its openness the geography hides the obvious, forces a different sort of attention for its wide spaces, and demands a watchfulness. Mystery is at the heart of such a country.

For me, the last piece in the puzzle was Tony Hillerman. We had spoken on the phone several times and exchanged a number of letters over the past two years. He always answered the phone the same way, snapping his name out—"Hillerman"—as if he had something else to do right away—and he probably did, considering the number of books he has written in the past twenty years. He was happy to talk about his work but reluctant to make a commitment to any definite time for a meeting. So when I left for New Mexico, I still was not sure I would track down Hillerman. After two years he was a mystery man to me in a number of ways.

A few days before I was to fly back east, I called him again. I heard the same gravelly editor's voice—"Hillerman." But this time he told me that the following afternoon he was going to be in Santa Fe at a "fancy school up there called St. John's College." Could I meet him there? As I recalled, Walker Percy had described Santa Fe as "the locus of pure possibility." That seemed a good omen, and the next morning I headed through Gallup, past Acoma Sky City and Mount Taylor, west into Albuquerque, and north to Santa Fe.

I met Hillerman in the hills around Santa Fe, where St. John's College rises above the adobe-filled landscape and art galleries in the center of town. He was coming to speak at the Bread Loaf School of English at St. John's, but somehow he didn't seem to fit the button-down atmosphere of the place. Hillerman is tall, an inch or so over six feet, but appears even bigger than he is because, like Hemingway, he's big all over, double chin and paunch, an inversion of that wedge-shaped body he so often describes in his Navajo characters. Like most of the Navajos he writes about, he's still a country boy, sporting an eleven-dollar watch and the vestiges of an Oklahoma twang. The black glasses that rest on his pointy nose when he reads were in the pocket of his blue short-sleeved shirt. The whole outfit, tan pants and homely black shoes, probably cost less than one of Tom Wolfe's handkerchiefs.

Our conversation about Navajos and his writing drifted amiably from office to classroom to plazita, starting in the early afternoon and ending about 10:30 at night as we sat in his wife's new Buick with the vanity light illuminating us in the darkness of the college parking lot. "Navajos have no word in their language for early and late," he said. "They look at time as a confluence. You'll meet someone at Gallup, and he'll show up half an hour after the established time. You'll say, 'You're late.' He'll respond, 'What's this about late? You're here, I'm here. What's the problem?'"

He waited a moment, Navajo style: "I've been fascinated with the culture for years. For a number of reasons. Speech is powerful, sacred for the Navajos. There is a tendency to think before one speaks. The listener leaves some space for thought. We find all this pretty strange in the white world. Their attitudes toward old people are different than ours. It's a matrilineal society. The woman owns the farm land, the man owns the religious paraphernalia. Living an isolated life, they tend to be very interested in people. They're friendly and they love laughter. I never met a Navajo who didn't enjoy a laugh"—he paused, tightening the strings of his Oklahoma twang—"usually at my expense."

"I'm a religious man," he continued. "When I meet up with other people who have a sense of the spiritual, I feel connected to them. Most Navajos are truly religious. They live their religion day in and day out. In an unusual way my Catholicism connects with their beliefs. But generally the role of man in our western origin stories is to master the planet. For many Indian tribes like the Navajos it is to take care of the world."

Hillerman had just been given the Ambassador Award by the Native American Council, and his sympathies were clear. "The history of our relationship with the Indian has been a long series of 'punitive expeditions'; that's what the United States government calls it when the Indians have land we want. It means go out there, kill Indians, and take their land. The ignorance of the American public about Native Americans is nearly impregnable. It's monolithic. Then, of course, there are the Eastern Libs. To them the Indians are special people, but of course they wouldn't want to associate with them. John Wayne shot us off our horses, but the Libs humiliated us."

I found it interesting that he used the word "us" to describe Native American culture. In his essay "Mystery, Country Boys, and the Big Reservation," he talked about the separation between the town boys and the country boys, between "them" and "us." He continues to make that distinction. His writing may have its origin in this conflict, in a desire to describe the mysterious spirit of the land and the country people who live on it.

"Writers were not real flesh and blood where I grew up when I was growing up," he said. "I read a lot but the writers didn't seem real. I was planning to be an engineer, but I was saved from that fate by an F in calculus. An A in English helped too. People didn't go to college where I grew up. They were rural poor. You hoped that the M.D. in town went to college, but you weren't sure. You just hoped. With some hard work and luck I got to go to college, and I got to write every day as a newspaperman about cops and politics and people. Kurt Vonnegut once said that you have to write about a million words of trash before you really get started. Newspaper work helps in that respect. For years, then, as a news writer I had been doing the hundred-yard dash, and although I wanted very much to do a marathon, I settled on the mile instead. Once I get the mystery mastered—I'm still working on it—then who knows? I've always wanted to write a redneck *Catcher in the Rye*, about a country kid who goes to an undistinguished land grant college in the West. I even got it started years ago, but I was smart enough to know I wasn't good enough to write it. But some day I think I will be. When I started out my agent didn't want to have anything to do with my work on the grounds that it might hurt her reputation. When I started to get published, they called my stuff mysteries—now they're called novels, and I guess I have to start taking myself seriously. Larry McMurtry had a T-shirt he wore back to the Big Apple recently: 'Minor Regional Novelist.'" He smiled at the thought of McMurtry strolling down Fifth Avenue with that T-shirt on.

"At first I was jumpy about the idea of writing about Navajos," he went on. "But I guess I've never been able to buy this idea that there are important racial differences. You can make this sexual as well. McMurtry's women characters are truer than his men. I don't think you have to be a woman to write about women or a Navajo to write about Navajos. Perhaps you gain some distance in writing about the 'other.' But, finally, my stories are about justice. I believe in law, but if you're a religious person there's always another law you obey first."

Like Jim Chee chasing a suspect into the night, I followed Tony Hillerman down the winding roads from St. John's, through the back roads of Santa Fe, and onto Route 23 toward Albuquerque. A few miles outside of

Santa Fe, he pulled onto the shoulder of the highway. We both got out of our cars and stared into the enveloping secret of the sky. He was stopping, generously, to point out the best and least expensive places to stay in the area, but he spent most of the time calling my attention to the full moon peeking coyly from behind black clouds and the dark, puzzling landscape that surrounded us. After all, it seemed, this was his true story. In his books the great mystery is the world itself.

CHAPTER 5

NEW JERSEY

In New Jersey, anything can happen.
                                    —Woody Allen,
                                    The Purple Rose of Cairo

*They [the Pine Barrens of New Jersey] seem to
be headed slowly toward extinction.*
                    —John McPhee, *The Pine Barrens*

Ted Gordon reminds me of a composite of all those actors who portrayed Charlie Chan in the movies. He has high cheekbones and scimitar-shaped eyes. He even has a slight lisp that sounds Oriental, the *r*'s blurring into *w*'s and *l*'s. By his own account, the fifty-five-year-old retired high school teacher long ago made the New Jersey Pine Barrens his "life's obsession."

He first saw the Pine Barrens when he was about eleven, in 1948, shortly after he arrived in the United States. He had spent his first ten years in Hockenheim, Germany, near Heidelberg in the Rhine Valley. After his father died in the war and his mother remarried, they moved to America. Although he did not grow up in the Pine Barrens, he took weekend and summer excursions into the area throughout his adolescence and into his young manhood. When he married and started a family, he moved into the wilderness that he had fallen in love with as a boy, and he has lived there for the past three decades.

John McPhee's book *The Pine Barrens* was published a few years after Ted Gordon moved into the wilds of New Jersey. When I read it for the first time about twenty-five years ago, it left an imprint on my imagination. I'm not exactly sure why. It was certainly more than a youthful admiring of his writing style, although clearly that was part of it. Perhaps, though, the book caught my imagination for the same reason the area caught Ted Gordon's: it was the search for some private place untouched by the world I saw every day. It might have had something to do with my growing up in the Bronx, squeezed in on all sides by apartment buildings and buses and people. My only rural escapes were brief hikes into the botanical gardens where I sat on the rusty banks of the Bronx River and occasionally, when my friends and I were daring enough, leaped into its murky depths. Other than summer trips to Maine, I knew of no countryside nearby, outside of what I could conjure in my imagination.

In *The Pine Barrens* McPhee showed me a retreat that was not too far away, a wilderness in the midst of the urban and suburban sprawl. It was difficult for me to believe that such a place existed, that another country was nearby, that, as McPhee wrote, "on a very clear night a bright light in the pines would be visible from the Empire State Building."

Having taken a circuitous route over a period of twenty-five years, I had finally gotten to the Pine Barrens, but now, after rereading the book, I wondered if the place any longer resembled McPhee's description of it. When he wrote the book, New Jersey had nearly one thousand people per square mile, the highest population density of any state in the union. In cramped corners of northern New Jersey there were as many as forty thousand people per square mile, but in many parts of the Pine Barrens there were only fifteen people per square mile. As McPhee pointed out, the Pine Barrens was the epicenter of a fast-growing megalopolis, an amorphous city that oozed its way from Boston to Richmond.

New Jersey still has the greatest population density of all the states, with close to one thousand and fifty people per square mile, far outdistancing its nearest rivals like Connecticut, Massachusetts, and even the congested Rhode Island. But the Pine Barrens, which is bigger than many national parks—more than ten times the size of Acadia National Park in Maine, larger than the Great Smoky Mountains National Park in North Carolina and Tennessee, and nearly as big as Yosemite—is still relatively unpopulated. Maureen McAnespy of the Pinelands Commission says that there is a range in population density in the area, anywhere from ten to four thousand people per square mile. But the heavily populated areas are all in Ocean County, in towns like Waretown and Tuckerton near the shore. Once you get away from the periphery of the Pines and move toward the center of the wilderness circle, towns like Hog Wallow and Chatsworth in Woodland Township, then the population thins and the trees thicken. According to Carol Cobb, the town clerk of Woodland Township, there are fewer than ten people per square mile in much of the heart of the Pine Barrens. "There are sections," she told me, "where you go for miles and miles without ever seeing a house. I've lived here since 1969 and there hasn't been much change in that time. The 1990 census says that our population decreased since 1980. As a matter of fact, in the past twenty-five years, since John McPhee's book was published, our population has remained pretty much perfectly stable." By that she means there are still about two thousand people in an approximately one hundred–square-mile area in Woodland Township, averaging a little over twenty people per square mile. In many of those square miles, as Cobb points out, a traveler would be hard pressed to find one or two people, let alone twenty.

Most people imagine New Jersey to be a small state veined by thousands of miles of highways knotting through shopping malls and factories and suburbs. That image is partially true, certainly, but there is also a wilderness heart to the state, a thousand–square-mile section of sandy pine and oak forests, dense cedar swamps, greenish-brown streams, and bogs aflame with orchids. In his book on the geography of New Jersey, Charles Stansfield, Jr., called it "a curiosity in the northeastern United States—an almost empty land, not mountainous and highly accessible from great cities." As Arthur Pierce has said in *Iron in the Pines*, "Few areas in the United States are so heavily traveled, yet so little known, as southern New Jersey." For most travelers the Pine Barrens are what they pass through on their way to the shore. For many, it is merely a flat stretch of rural road between Philadelphia and Atlantic City. It is not *a place* but *a way* to someplace else.

It is also one of the most controversial areas in the state—a botanist's wonderland, a developer's dream, a naturalist's last stand. In the late 1960s there was a grand plan to build the largest airport in the world in the Pine Barrens, much larger than Newark, La Guardia, and Kennedy airports combined. The plan called for supersonic jets and a shining new city of a quarter of a million people. However, in 1979 New Jersey passed the Pinelands Protection Act, resulting in the designation of over one million acres as land in which development was strictly controlled. The "preservation area" is the heart of the Pine Barrens, and within those roughly four hundred thousand acres development is virtually prohibited. The "protection area" also carefully regulates growth but the restrictions within its approximately one million acres are less severe. Finally, there is the Pinelands National Preserve, slightly over one million acres with broader and fewer restrictions on development. Most of the preserve lands are on the periphery of the Pine Barrens, leaving the thousand-square-mile heart remarkably pristine.

Over one hundred million years ago the Pine Barrens was much more densely populated, but with fish, not people. The area was ocean then. As the sea level fluctuated over the millennia, the landscape changed from ocean to lagoons to salt marshes. What was left was a coarse, sandy soil with layers of impermeable clay deep below the surface. Abundant rainfall in southern New Jersey, along with the top layers of porous soil, created a vast reservoir of water, an aquifer as pure as one could imagine and as vulnerable to pollution as one would suspect.

The sandy soil of the Pine Barrens, which creates the aquifer, is highly acidic and not good for farming, but it is perfect for blueberry and huckleberry fields and cranberry bogs. It is also perfect for fires because of its dry surface soil and resinous pines. There are over one thousand fires in the Barrens each year, but the vegetation has adapted to the difficult conditions, with stands of pitch pines and miles of dwarf forests. The people have adapted, as well, making a way of life in an area that McPhee described as "another country," a separate world of vanished towns, buried history, tar paper cabins, and singular human beings.

THE PRESENT

> *. . . the relationship between this father and son*
> *is as attractive as anything I have seen in*
> *Alaska—both of them self-reliant beyond the*
> *usual reach of the term, the characteristic formed*
> *by this country. Whatever they are doing,*
> *whether it is mining or something else, they do*
> *for themselves what no one else is here to do for*
> *them. Their kind is more endangered every year.*
> —John McPhee,
> *Coming Into the Country*

John McPhee's heroes are usually ordinary people. His landscape can be Alaska or New Jersey, Nevada or Switzerland, the orange groves of Florida or the rivers of northern Maine. The geography is not exotic; we pass by such places all the time without paying attention, perhaps only giving a glance as we hurtle through at sixty miles per hour. The McPhee hero could be our next door neighbor, the one we just never really noticed. The McPhee territory could be that piece of land that looked marginally interesting but that we never took time to investigate. As William Marvel of the *Detroit News* said, "John McPheeland is a small nation populated almost entirely by canoe makers, basketball players, inspired tinkerers, backyard inventors, restaurateurs, vegetable growers, and geologists. In John McPheeland all the people still care about what they do and they do it exceedingly well." And, as another critic wrote, "The essence of McPhee's fascination with the actual world is revealed in his attachment to character."

From his first book, *A Sense of Where You Are*, in 1965, a profile of the basketball player Bill Bradley, to his recent *Looking for a Ship*, which focuses on merchant mariner Captain Washburn, McPhee writes about people who are, in a sense, reflections of himself. They are craftsmen, and McPhee is drawn toward skillful people, toward people who thrive in relative anonymity. As Larry McMurty said about McPhee, "Skills absorb him; the attempt to describe them accurately prompts his most intense concentration." McPhee is a writer who views structure as a ceramicist views a mass of clay: he sculpts it with the utmost care, shaping and crafting his materials until all the separate pieces are whole. Like the people he writes about, McPhee is also thriving in something resembling seclusion. He is not shy and he does grant a rare interview, but his photograph does not appear on his book jackets and he does not hit the talk-show circuit with each new book. Nor does he do a round of lucrative readings on college campuses each year. Instead, he writes in his office on the Princeton campus until eight o'clock or so each night and then returns home to have dinner with his wife, Yolanda, a horticulturist whose job also demands that she work late. He shuns most publicity and concentrates on the work. When he is not at home, he is off gathering material for another story—always about interesting individuals, not necessarily odd or eccentric but always *individual*, fascinating and fascinated by the world, knowledgeable, curious, able. McPhee writes about intricate processes—designing canoes, playing tennis, selling produce, building airplanes—but it is the people who attempt to control the processes that truly interest him. It is those strong, engaged human beings that he seeks in his travels into the world outside of Princeton. Robert Coles, in writing about *Coming Into the Country*, touches on the center of all of McPhee's work: "Those human creatures McPhee stalks—diminutive as in a Japanese or Chinese painting against the largeness of the land, the water, the hills, the trees—have their own ironic grandeur. To face down a demanding, consuming external world is to be on to something psychologically, spiritually—existence converging toward essence."

Having written twenty-two books in the past twenty-eight years, McPhee is recognized as one of the premier nonfiction writers alive. Along with Tom Wolfe, Gay Talese, and Joan Didion, he is always mentioned in any discussion about influential creative journalists. But as far as sheer variety and consistent productivity are concerned, he stands alone. He has written on a dizzying array of subjects, everything from museum directors and produce markets to natural disasters and rural doctors in Maine. Perhaps for a man who has come to be known as something of a literary explorer, who journeys into the wilds of Alaska or New Jersey, floats on the Great Salt Lake in Utah, rides the back roads of Georgia looking for roadkill, Princeton is the perfect point of departure. He was born and raised in Princeton, and he has lived there most of his adult life. It is a charming university town, quaint, perhaps a bit too gentrified for some long-time residents. It is surely a world apart from the Newarks and Patersons that most people associate with the soul of the state. As William Howarth pointed out in his introduction to *The John McPhee Reader*, Princeton is the "epicenter of [McPhee's] cartography, and its character defines most of his interests." Its character, according to Howarth, is varied and particularly American, but even more significant, perhaps, is the town's elegant stability, like the calm, ordered prose that graces McPhee's stories.

McPhee graduated from Princeton University and spent a year abroad studying literature and playing basketball at Cambridge University, but his dream was to write for *The New Yorker*. When he was eighteen he decided that he would one day write a long fact piece for the magazine. For the next fourteen years he collected rejection slips from *The New Yorker*, wrote television scripts, and became a staff reporter for *Time* magazine. In 1963, at the age of thirty-two, he received his first acceptance from *The New Yorker* for "Basketball and Beefeaters," a story about his adventures playing basketball in the Tower of London and other unusual spots in Great Britain. Not long after that, William Shawn, then editor of *The New Yorker*, offered McPhee a position as a staff writer.

During the past three decades, as a writer for the

magazine, McPhee has defined the contours of the non-fiction story as much as E. B. White did the personal essay or John Cheever the lyrical work of short fiction. At first glance, the subjects he writes about might appear uninviting—oranges or teachers or rocks—but in the smooth lines of his prose and the perfectly framed constructions of his stories, the reader finds an eloquence and subtle humor, a dynamic exploration of character, and in most of his work a sense of American individuality. As Ronald Weber said of his work, it always "seeks beyond the flow of fact."

> *During his four collegiate years [McPhee] appeared on "Twenty Questions," a weekly television and radio program originating from New York. The producers wanted one young person on the show's panel. Fond of games he rapidly mastered the art of identifying mystery items—animal, vegetable, or mineral—with questions that could be answered Yes or No. The training was probably useful for a future journalist; it taught him how to assemble facts and infer their hidden meanings.*
>
> —William Howarth,
> *The John McPhee Reader*

Today the facts I seek come from John McPhee. This is our second meeting. We met once earlier in the summer

New Jersey

to discuss plans for my project on the New Jersey Pine Barrens, a return to the place twenty-five years after his account, using his book as an imaginative guide. Now we will speak about his work in general, for somehow I feel that knowing the man better will help me to understand myself as a writer, as well as my reasons for wanting to explore in particular the territory re-created in *The Pine Barrens*.

The room is longer than a monk's cell but not much wider. It even has the requisite ascetic's cot, narrow and uncomfortable looking. The corridor outside is bland and featureless, and the doors are made of the sort of pressboard that would probably splinter under a loud "Amen." But even though East Pyne Building has the stony elegance of a medieval monastery, it's actually the center for humanities on Princeton University's campus and is where on most days for twelve hours or so John McPhee uses that cot in room 311 to "work horizontally," writing on a clipboard until "everything tumbles into the right slot."

Perhaps more consistently and dramatically than any other nonfiction writer today, McPhee has been able to find the right slot, producing over twenty critically acclaimed books in little more than a quarter of a century. At sixty-one years old, he is still slim and athletic, and although after an Achilles tendon injury a few years ago he no longer plays basketball or tennis, he still rides his bicycle when he's not off marching with the Swiss army, standing aboard a merchant marine vessel, or roaming the geological backroads of America. The final book in his quartet on geology, *Assembling California*, is about to be published. He has just read the galleys and is already involved in another project about the cattle business in Utah.

A handwritten sign over the inside of his office door reads, "My patience is not inexhaustible," but my suspicion is that patience may be a big part of his genius. In conversation, as in his books, McPhee is a lover of small details. He is the kind of man who draws intricate directions on the backs of cocktail napkins. He is a connoisseur of topographic maps, a passionate list maker, a reverent collector of facts. He seems to have as much patience with people as he does with the materials he shapes into his stories. Of course, he's not an easy man to get in touch with—no one who has written a book virtually every year since he was in his mid-thirties can have much time for anything but writing or family (four daughters by his first marriage and four stepchildren). For this meeting I have in mind a *Paris Review* style of interview, a question-and-answer format, and I have specific things to ask him. Because I feel lucky to have the chance to speak with him, to catch him for the second time between travel and writing, I don't even murmur dissent when he says he doesn't want me to use a tape recorder. "This is strictly a professional decision," he says. "You'll get a better story without a tape recorder. Besides, the question-and-answer format is the most primitive form of writing, you realize. Writing is selection. It's better to start choosing right here and right now."

However, he tells me that, despite the myth that he never uses such machines, he uses tape recorders "with some frequency." He uses them when a person speaks so rapidly or technically that it is difficult to get the words otherwise. He used a tape recorder in his conversations with Captain Washburn, for instance, and made that clear in *Looking for a Ship*, a book about the United States Merchant Marines. Finally, though, he feels that such machines have a tendency to "slavishly reproduce Bushisms," and he seems happy to tell me about the reporter who interviewed him some years back—with a tape recorder. The reporter didn't bother to take notes, and McPhee got a call that night. "The man was in a deep gloom. The machine hadn't recorded anything."

Therefore, as I hesitate for a moment in front of East Pyne, the stone archways looking like the entrance to a forbidding castle, I can't stop myself from having some serious doubts about interviewing a writer who has been described by one reviewer as a man with "total recall." I check my bag—three pens, two notebooks, questions, extra batteries for the tape recorder left behind—and bound down the hall, past television newscaster Roger Mudd, who is having a conference with a student, and knock on 311. The man who answers the door is slight, but there is nothing fragile about him. He looks like a man who might have recently explored

Alaska, traveled through the orange groves in Florida, or canoed the rivers of northern Maine. He has dark gray hair, a slightly grayer beard, and a healthy, weathered face. Canted ever so slightly to the right, his glasses sit a bit crookedly on his nose. His eyes are clear, and although the skin underneath is laced with lines, their smiling aspect seems to dismiss the possibility of weariness. He is dressed casually, in an orderly disarray— corduroy pants, a faded green shirt, black socks, and brown walking shoes. It's hard to imagine him in a white suit, à la Tom Wolfe, or on the talk show circuit, like Truman Capote, or loudly proclaiming his character, in the blaring tones of Norman Mailer. He seems more like Joan Didion, inconspicuous. It's possible to see how his description of Frank L. Boyden in *The Headmaster* might fit him as well: "People walk right by him sometimes without seeing him."

His office seems to fit him, too. It is casual and unpretentious but neat and organized even in its motley look. On one wall is a physical map of the world, on another a tectonic map of North America, and on another a series of geological maps with a sign—"Public toilet 440 years"—thumbtacked over it. The far end of the room looks like a version of Fred Brown's yard in *The Pine Barrens*—a small refrigerator, an ancient typewriter, a coffee maker—but unlike Brown's collection, everything here seems in good working order. "At one time," McPhee says, "I had the idea that the room where you worked on a piece of writing would be filled exclusively with stuff related to what you were working on, covering the walls."

"But," he goes on, looking at the pictures of his family and the memorabilia from friends and various assignments, "that's been violated more than once, as you can see." However, the room seems less a violation than a representation of the man. There are a number of desks and bookcases bridging one end of the room and the other, and a cot with papers placed in carefully separated piles—letters from his publisher, a note pad from *The New Yorker*, even a paperback copy of *The Pine Barrens* lying there as if it's waiting for me to pick it up. The dictionary on the desk near the door just happens to be open to the phrase "legal cap," and a sign near the ceiling warns:

Danger
Bear Trap
Do Not Approach

Clearly the private and public man are entwined in all this—in the photographs of Captain Washburn standing alone or Bill Bradley towering over McPhee, in the canvas bags with "Princeton English Department" or "Department of Geology/Princeton University" printed on them, in the picture of his daughter Laura with the inscription "Portrait of the Artist as a Young(ish) Teacher." A metal statue of a basketball player and a plastic cube with photographs of his daughters serve as bookends for a shelf of books by former students. There is a separate bookcase for works of nonfiction that he uses in the course he teaches at Princeton titled The Literature of Fact: *In Cold Blood, Joe Gould's Secret, Blue Highways, Let Us Now Praise Famous Men, Armies of the Night, Hiroshima, The Right Stuff, In Patagonia, Five Seasons, The Sea Around Us, The Soul of the New Machine*, and others. The first book on the shelf, *Alive*, and the last, *The Journalist and the Murderer*, are both, ironically it seems, about forms of cannibalism and perhaps the pitfalls of writing nonfiction.

But, as McPhee sits back in his chair, hands behind his head and feet propped up on his desk, his voice is calm and self-assured. He gives his beard a meditative scratch and takes his time, mulling things over and structuring his ideas like the pieces of one of his stories. He answers in a voice that is rasping and slightly nasal but pleasant, with just a whisper of his New Jersey upbringing; its rough lyrical clarity seems perfectly tuned for communicating long passages of information. And behind every sentence, pushing each vowel and consonant out a fraction faster than you would expect, is the source of McPhee's writing: a curiosity about the world and a boyish exuberance about what he has learned out there.

I wish I hadn't asked my first question as soon as it leaves my mouth: *Many critics see* Coming Into the Country *as your best work. What do you see as the best things you've done?* His warm eyes grow a little cool, and he appears to glance at the "Bear Trap" sign. "I find this sort of question mildly irritating," he says. "There seems to be a need in people to use words like 'best.'" He looks out the window as if he's trying to locate the individuals who do this kind of thing. I'm glad he doesn't direct his gaze at me. "I'm pleased with *Coming Into the Country*, but it's not my 'best' work. I've received letters from readers about each of my books saying *Oranges* or *Giving Good Weight* or whatever was their favorite. Each one is unique, itself. You do your best with the materials that you have to work with in each piece or you don't turn it in. You can't compare *The Deltoid Pumpkin Seed* and *Looking for a Ship*. I wouldn't differentiate between them any more than I would compare my daughters." He pauses over this thought and cocks his head to the right as if he's looking for another angle. "Nonfiction writers go out not knowing what to expect. In a way you're like a cook foraging for materials, and in many ways, like a cook, you're only as good as your materials. You go out looking for characters to sketch, arresting places to describe, dialogue to capture—the way you would gather berries. You hope for the greatest variety. Perhaps the work that best exemplifies what I'm talking about, this sort of variety, is *The Deltoid Pumpkin Seed*. I'm not saying it's the 'best,' but it is a good example of what I reach for in my writing."

I glance down at those lonely batteries, lying like two displaced persons in my bag, and ask him about the critic who suggested he had total recall. "I don't have it," he says simply. "Truman Capote said that when he was working on *In Cold Blood* he trained himself to listen in the day and remember that night exactly what people said." Once again he pauses and the lines around his eyes thread together as he smiles. "Good for him! That's a dazzling skill. It's no skill, though, that I'd associate with a normal human being." He reaches into the shadows of the bookcase next to him and takes out three small note pads and fans them in the air. "I write in notebooks like these. If I interview you, you know what I'm doing. I make it clear to you, what I'm working on, where it's going to be published. My notebook is always visible, a factor between us. It's like a film crew, only less obtrusive." I wonder aloud about a particular passage from *Coming Into the Country*, asking how he recorded a long conversation with John Kauffman as they paddled along an Alaskan river. "That's easy," he tells me. "He paddled. I wrote . . . fast."

I decide to push a bit further in the same direction and mention William Howarth's idea from *The John McPhee Reader* that creating a true replica of an informant's conversation demanded a ventriloquist's skill. Then I quote Kathy Smith's interpretation of his work in *Literary Journalism in the Twentieth Century*: "McPhee's fictionalizing act, whether he acknowledges it or not, is grounded in the same logic as all narrative, one that seeks, through illusion, a perfect apprehension of the world." I can tell he doesn't like this question any more than he did my first one, but this time we both glance out the window, as if we might catch a glimpse of this nefarious Kathy Smith. When he looks at me, he says, "That's just academic air. Of course, there's definite truth in it, the idea that all writing is fiction. I agree with the idea if you express it in a certain way. You can't exactly reproduce human life; everything is a little bit of illusion. So what? Ho, hum. Basically, the whole thing is academic air. Everyone knows that at the start. The important gradation in the whole thing is that you get as close as you can to what you saw and heard."

What about works like In Cold Blood *or* The Electric Kool-Aid Acid Test? *In your discussion with Norman Sims in* The Literary Journalists *you say, "You don't make up dialogue. . . . And you don't get inside their heads and think for them." Have Capote, Wolfe, and others gone too far?*

"I greatly admire *In Cold Blood*, especially in terms of structure, particularly the first three quarters. But it falls apart, for me, at the conclusion, kind of like a burlap bag spilling grain at the end. But on the matter of the dialogue, clearly I have my doubts that you can train yourself to remember verbatim hours later." About Tom Wolfe all he will say is that he is a stylistic marvel, "interesting, funny." But about *creating* characters in nonfiction, he is direct: "Nonfiction writers have a real debt to one another and to their readers. When that *Washington Post* reporter won the Pulitzer Prize a few years back for a story that turned out to be a complete fiction, she did the whole business a serious disservice. The debt we owe to one another in this form of writing has to do with credibility. Nonfiction writing is like an aquifer: one pollutant can spread through it and taint it all."

One of the four calls he receives during our conversation interrupts our talk now; all of them, some from other writers, he handles with tact and care, but each time he explains that he is busy speaking with me right now. I've been doing what any book lover does sitting in a person's office waiting for him to get off the phone: I eye the titles in the bookcase. When he hangs up the receiver, I ask him if he has read William Least Heat-Moon's new book *Prairy Erth*. He tells me that he admires it a great deal, that "it was a good choice to go deep this time." He says, "Bill is a friend of mine, and I feel guilty that I haven't written him yet to tell him how much I like the book, the stories of the people he found."

It seems natural to ask him about the people he writes about in his books, those individuals the critics call the "McPhee heroes," people like Fred Brown in *The Pine Barrens* or the Gelvins in *Coming Into the Country*. "I write about real people in real places," he says. "All of my work is about that. It's not the unusual person that is most interesting—the eccentric. I don't have any predilection about that. In Alaska there are lots of unusual people. But within the context of Alaska the Gelvins are not unusual or eccentric or odd. I remember saying to myself as I worked on *Coming Into the Country* that if I don't succeed in describing them, in capturing their character, then the whole thing will fall apart. They were the real McCoy: they were so *uneccentric*. Fred Brown, too, was the solid stuff of the place where he lived."

McPhee's skill over the years has been in taking that solid stuff of the world and shaping it into narratives, and I ask him about William Howarth's description of his method of composition that appears in the introduction to *The John McPhee Reader*. *Is structure, as Howarth suggests, the main ingredient in your work? Have advances in computer technology changed your methods?*

"The reader is not necessarily conscious of structure," he says. "Readers are not supposed to be aware of structure. But the logic may bring them in. My computer has been adapted to what I did before. There is a computer genius at Princeton—Howard Strauss—who has written programs to do the same thing I did in the tenth century, when I started writing. One of his programs implodes information, the other explodes it. I've told him: if he leaves Princeton, I leave too . . . I still do note cards, though. I move them around until I get them in the right order. I write the lead first, then work on the rest. And I always know what the ending is going to be. This may sound mechanistic, but it liberates you to write."

As if the world "liberate" has triggered his memory, he stands up and suggests we go to the Annex to have lunch. We pass Roger Mudd and walk for five minutes across campus through a sea of dappled leaves and past strolling students. The restaurant is an unpretentious place in the basement of a building that stands near the intersection of Nassau and Tulane Streets. Across the street is the Midlantic Bank, in the brick building where McPhee once had his office over a hardware store. In that rented office he wrote *Coming Into the Country* and a number of other books. Next door to the Annex is the Rialto Barber Shop, where McPhee gets his hair cut and his beard trimmed. On the wall near the front door is a faded 1975 newspaper photograph of a beardless McPhee, a handsome, square face. When Ed Cifelli, one of the owners of the barber shop, sees me looking at it he says, "He won't shave off his beard. His wife likes it. He's afraid if he shaves it off she's gonna leave him." The other barber, Rich Pinelli, tells me to look at the drawing of the Midlantic Bank Building that is hanging on the far wall. "That's where he had his office, you know. He wrote about everything up there—oranges, canoes— but never about barbers. We're too boring." I have to say the drawing is interesting—well, not so much the drawing as the postcards that almost completely cover it—naked women from Aruba, Florida, Hawaii, and other tropical paradises. It seems that these barbers, like McPhee, have a diverse sense of adventure.

In the Annex we find a quiet spot, a few tables away from a group of cartoonists, one of whom—Henry Martin—regularly contributes to *The New Yorker*. The restaurant reminds me of Walker Percy's description of Princeton in *The Last Gentleman*: everyone seemed to have "a certain Princeton way of talking . . . and a certain way of sticking their hands in their pockets and setting their chins in their throats." There is a club atmosphere, but, as Percy says, a "muted Yankee friendliness" too. I follow McPhee's lead and order a turkey club sandwich, but not even my admiration for his writing skill or his gentle humanity can induce me to order, as he does, the lima bean soup.

I ask him about the writing course he teaches at Princeton, The Literature of Fact. It is a course that he has taught once every year or so as the Ferris Professor of Journalism since 1975. I wonder how he gets his students to view things differently, to enhance their powers of seeing. "Nothing that I know of directly," he says, looking into the swampy-green bowl in front of him. "I tell them that I'm not a real professor. I'm a writer, brought here by the university to look at the writing that they do. I look over their shoulder at what they do and they can look over mine at what I do. As far as being observant is concerned, I am observant when I have a notebook in my hand. But when I'm not working, that part of me shuts off. As a matter of fact, my family teases me about my not noticing things. Six elephants could walk through the kitchen, they say, and I'd never notice."

A bit later he says, "Writing teaches writing. Writing begets writing. It doesn't make any difference what the form is as long as the person who talks to the students about it is interested in their writing and knows something about the genre." *Do you read the reviews of your work?* I'm thinking in particular of Edward Hoagland's 1975 *New York Times Book Review* criticism of McPhee that he didn't take enough risks. "I read them. Usually I ask Farrar to collect them and send me a batch. That way I place them in a larger context. But I can't say that I've read anything in a review that caused a great swerve in my writing. I've seen everything from soup to nuts, from highly intelligent comments to truly dumb remarks. If you are a writer and you are reading reviews of your work, you have a unique view of the process—reviewers, you see, are doing a sketch of themselves. Therefore, it's not a good idea, generally speaking, to let any of them be a pilot fish for your work."

Who, then, is your ideal reader? I remind him of John Cheever's teasing response to the same question in which he offered height, weight, and other specifics. "Cheever's was a creative and humorous response to a pretty amorphous question," he says and pauses to choose his words. "Obviously, many of the people who will be reading what I write will be smarter, more sensitive, more subtle than I am. I know that when I'm writing. I write with them in mind. You often have a problem when you are trying to describe something and you know some readers will know all about it in advance while others will not. You have to find a way to negotiate this road—especially when you're writing about science. One way to do it is to get at the information through children: for instance, to write something like—'When Ted was sixteen he learned about particles in physics.' Bring it in through characters, through what interested or inspired them."

For his own inspiration, McPhee draws on the things that interested him before he was twenty. "Much of it came from Camp Keewaydin in Vermont, eight miles south of Middlebury," he tells me. "A few years back I was giving a talk at Vassar and a young man raised his hand and asked me what academic institution had influenced me the most. Well, I had gone to Princeton High School and Princeton University and Cambridge, but I didn't hesitate for a second. I said Keewaydin; it was a real educational institution. I started going there in the summers when I was six, and I was working as a camp counselor when I was in college. There are lots of good ideas for pieces of writing, but you still have to sell them. Someone has to want them, and it's far more likely that something you have an emotional commitment to will work out than some Hessian piece of writing."

I bring up having recently seen a *New Yorker* video in which he mentions that he invents ways to avoid writing, until the pressure builds up and some words leak out. I wonder if he's ever thought of shedding the "lonely, nerve-wracking" writing activity to do something else. I'm thinking particularly of the conclusion of the essay he wrote about the ranger in Maine named John McPhee whom he met a few years ago. The writer ends up "wishing he were John McPhee."

Once again he confirms that there is no other profession that he is genuinely drawn toward and says that his daughter Jenny tells him that he overemphasizes the negative aspects of the daily life of a writer. "There are many rewards," he says. "Making something that you have a compulsion to make and being glad when it's done. At least a few months later you're glad. The biggest reward for me is that those books of mine exist. I'm still a little bit surprised and awfully pleased that people seem to like them."

And, of course, many people do, among them some of the most gifted younger practitioners of literary journalism. I bring up Tracy Kidder's and Mark Kramer's citing his influence on their work and ask about influences on his. But he won't name individual books or writers. He received a B.A. in English from Princeton and read English literature at Cambridge, but as a teenager it was the long fact pieces that drew him to *The New Yorker*. "But I didn't rule out anything as a younger writer," he explains. "I tried everything, sometimes with hilarious results. I think that young writers have to roll around like oranges on a conveyor belt. They have to try it all. If they are lucky, they'll fall into the right hole. There are plenty of writers in the wrong holes, that's for sure. Even with my reading, I take whatever the hell comes along. I read haphazardly and usually in the dead of night. I've taken in the last few years to listening to books on tape as I drive my car. Now, my ignition comes on, and a voice comes on with it."

Just as he finishes his sentence, a tweedy-looking, gray-haired gentleman comes up to our table, says "Hi, John," and relates a story about an aunt with Alzheimer's. "That's a story you should write about," he says as he waves goodbye.

"Do you get that suggestion often?" I ask him.

"Sure," he replies, then shrugs. "But he's just an English professor."

As we walk up the stairs toward a sunny, brisk afternoon, I ask him about a profile written a few years ago that described him as a "slightly eccentric recluse with a beard."

"Does that sound right?" I ask.

"It's perfect," he says and smiles.

"So, is it some eccentricity that keeps your photograph off your book jackets?"

"Actually, that's a complicated thing," he says. "I think authors can get between the reader and the work. A piece of writing is something in which the figure of the author is just one component. When I see this figure of author on television, for instance, coming between the reader and the work, I think the reader loses something. The reader is the most creative thing in a piece of work. The writer puts down the words and the reader creates a scene. Writing is literally in the eye of the beholder. Therefore, the writer who is embedded in the text can distract the reader by coming forward."

"Do you feel any kinship with the new journalists or the practitioners of creative nonfiction?"

"I'm not one of the new journalists. I'm an old journalist. I have some sympathy for the term 'creative nonfiction,' however. It's an attempt to sort out the too-numerous things that will be placed under the same category—everything from the telephone book and an instructional manual to the work of Joseph Mitchell. It's an attempt to recognize something, that a piece of writing can be creative while using factual materials, that creative work can respect fact."

We stand for a few more minutes on the corner of Tulane and Nassau, discussing the new *New Yorker*, the possible effects of Tina Brown's editorship, but he is reserving judgment, hoping that the magazine will nurture new writers the way it nurtured him.

"Things have always been allowed to grow there and not grow to fit the circumstances," he says. "A piece of writing is a piece of writing, whether it's a haiku or *The Anglo-Saxon Chronicle*, but when I started at the magazine I never had the onerous sense that my stories had to fit a mold. They had to be as long as they had to be and not a smidgen more. If that changes, *The New Yorker* will not be the same kind of seedbed. If that's the case, I feel sorry for younger writers."

Just one final question before the light turns green and he heads back onto the Princeton campus: "How does it feel to have the tables turned, to be interviewed rather than do the interviewing?"

New Jersey

"Well," he says, as he begins to cross the street, heading back toward the monk's cell with the cot, "anything beats writing."

> *A visitor who stays awhile in the Pine Barrens soon feels that he is in another country, where attitudes and ambitions are at a variance with the American norm. People who drive around in the pines and see houses like Fred Brown's, with tarpaper peeling from the walls, and automobiles overturned in the front yard, often decide, as they drive on, that they have just looked destitution in the face. I wouldn't call it that. I have yet to meet anyone living in the Pine Barrens who has in any way indicated envy of people who live elsewhere.*
>
> —John McPhee, *The Pine Barrens*

Within half an hour south of Princeton, I have wound my way onto Route 206 and touched the bristling edge of the Pine Barrens. Mist rises like smoke off the cranberry bogs, and the sun knifes through the hard, cold air lighting the sand, rocks, and forests with silver and bronze. In another twenty minutes I am in Chatsworth, in Woodland Township, what McPhee called the principal community in the area. "It is six miles north of the approximate center of the pines at Hog Wallow," he wrote, "and is surrounded on all sides by deep forest.

The town consists of three hundred and six people, seventy-four houses, ten trailers, a firehouse, a church, a liquor store, a post office, a school, two sawmills, and one general store." The town is much the same as he described it twenty-five years ago, and it is in the general store, Buzby's, that I wait for Ted Gordon, who will guide me around the area.

In Buzby's I briefly get the impression that this is more than another country; it is another time, as well. If it weren't for a few silent video games in the corner I could imagine that the late twentieth century had evaporated. A young boy sits at one of the tables, idly fingering the red-checked tablecloth, staring out the window as if he might be looking for the local truant officer. But soon other youngsters show up to wait in the warmth of the store for the school bus. They mill about, nudging one another, eyeing the candy in the glass cases as if they were surveying jewels that they might purchase. Some have the cash. Others look on enviously. A few more people sweep in, bringing gusts of cold air with them each time the door opens. A middle-aged man in a green jacket with yellow lettering that says "New Jersey Forest Fire Service" sits at one of the tables across from an angular young man with a bushy beard and a sweatshirt that reads "Piney Power." A smiling old-timer, wearing a hot pink baseball cap with "Miami Hurricanes" stitched into it, walks in to a chorus of "Hello, Cliff."

This is not the set for the television show "Cheers,"

but it may reflect some of the conflicting impulses created by change in the area. Buzby's, now one hundred years old, is no longer owned by the Buzbys. It is operated, as one Chatsworth resident told me, by "outlanders." The sign outside that reads "2 hot dogs for 99¢" has a story behind it, he tells me. "It seems like a good buy, eh," he says, "but it all came about because these new people who bought the place a few years ago (they're nothing like the Buzbys) decided that the little girl across the street who was selling hot dogs at the intersection to raise money to go to college was cutting into their business. The new owners decided they had to compete, went to court to get her to stop. They couldn't. Now she's off at college. And they sell hot dogs two for ninety-nine cents. You think they're making any money on that?"

When Ted Gordon arrives in his jeep to take me on a tour, my first question is about Bear Swamp Hill Fire Tower, the vantage point from which John McPhee opened his account in *The Pine Barrens*:

> From the fire tower on Bear Swamp Hill, in Washington Township, Burlington County, New Jersey, the view usually extends about twelve miles. To the north, forest land reaches to the horizon. The trees are mainly oaks and pines, and the pines predominate. Occasionally, there are long, dark, serrated stands of Atlantic white cedars, so tall and so closely set that they seem to be spread against the sky on the ridges of hills, when in

fact they grow along streams that flow through the forest. To the east, the view is similar, and few people who are not native to the region can discern essential differences from the high cabin of the fire tower, even though one difference is that huge areas out in this direction are covered with dwarf forests, where a man can stand among the trees and see for miles over their uppermost branches. To the south, the view is twice broken slightly—by a lake and by a cranberry bog—but otherwise it, too, goes to the horizon in forest. To the west, pines, oaks, and cedars continue all the way, and the western horizon includes the summit of another hill— Apple Pie Hill—and the outline of another fire tower, from which the view three hundred and sixty degrees around is virtually the same as the view from Bear Swamp Hill, where, in a moment's sweeping glance, a person can see hundreds of square miles of wilderness.

But, as Ted Gordon tells me, the fire tower at Bear Swamp Hill is no longer there. It was obliterated, exploded into fragments, in the early 1970s when an Air National Guard jet went out of control and decapitated the tower. The plane left a notch in the hill where it topped all the trees in its fatal descent. The fire tower at Apple Pie Hill is still working, though, and we will finish our explorations there in the late afternoon.

As we drive south toward Hog Wallow—the approximate center of the Pine Barrens—Gordon twists his trimmed graying beard, which is a few strands beyond being a Vandyke, and complains, "The Pine Barrens have definitely contracted. Many houses have been built in the last decade. On the eastern edge, especially, many inroads have been made by leisure villages." However, as we head toward the cranberry bogs there is no evidence of developers or retirement villages. From what I can tell, Hog Wallow is nothing more than a road with cranberry bogs alongside it.

We stop to watch the workers, like silhouettes against the pale day, walk through Haines Cranberry Bog. In general, cranberry bogs are sand-covered flatlands that can be flooded or drained when necessary. Flooding protects the vines from killing frosts and destructive insects. In this area, workers open up sluice gates, allowing water to enter from reservoirs on the upper stream system. The bogs are slightly slanted so that the canal system is gravity fed. The vines become slightly buoyant. Workers use an "egg beater" type of machine to agitate the water and separate the berries from the vines. Then the men come in with plastic or wooden booms and corral them to where a truck is waiting. A conveyor belt is placed in the bog, and the berries bounce along into the truck like tiny spaldeens.

We watch the men pushing the beaters through the calf-high crimson water in their boots and rubberized overalls. It's a cold morning and most of them wear hoods or hats. They push the agitators through the bog in a straight line. One man, like Moses with a four-foot staff in his right hand, leads them through the water, keeping them on the right track, back and forth, back and forth, across this red sea.

Just down a dirt road a short distance from the bog is Fred Brown's old place. John McPhee said in his book that it was his thirst and the water pump in the yard that first attracted his attention. But it was something of a wonder, McPhee said, that he ever noticed the pump at all because there was so much camouflage: "Among other things, eight automobiles in the yard, two of them on their sides and one of them upside down, all ten years old or older. Around the cars were old refrigerators, vacuum cleaners, partly dismantled radios, cathode-ray tubes, a short wooden ski, a large wooden mallet, dozens of cranberry picker's boxes, many tires, an orange crate dated 1946, a cord or so of firewood, mandolins, engine heads, and maybe a thousand other things." In McPhee's book Fred Brown became the central character, a sinewy, tough old bird, at the same time idiosyncratic and representative of the Pine Barrens. McPhee told me that he spent about eight months exploring the area, traveling the forty miles from Princeton with a sleeping bag or tent, spending days or weekends over that period. When he had collected his material, had gathered all his notes, he sat down at home and asked himself in a mild kind of panic, "What the devil do I do with all this stuff? The canvas was so miscellaneous. I was absolutely blocked. So I lay down on a picnic table in the backyard and stared at the leaves. I lay there for about two weeks. Then it dawned on me: make Fred Brown the organizing principle."

Fred Brown died a few years ago, but his house is still here, and except for a few minor details it is a still life of McPhee's description. I count only five cars—two Fords, a Studebaker, a Chrysler, and a Dodge—all rusted and most of them used as storage bins for old clothes and an assortment of items. A black cat perches on the fender of the Dodge, and a crew of its cousins eyes us from the tangle of vines and tree stumps. The Studebaker, with shadows of leaves swaying against it like waving hands, has a sign on the passenger's side window: "Drug Free Zone."

As we stand there, a man, the image of Fred Brown, opens the cabin door. Emile Brown, Fred's seventy-something-year-old son, looks like his father, except perhaps that Fred Brown in his mid-eighties looked younger than his son does now, and Emile's smile is not as wide or open as his father's appeared in photographs. But he seems to have the same elfish grin, even if his is toothless, and the same grey stubble. A faded brown plaid shirt sneaks beneath his green wind-breaker. His eyes stay somewhat veiled beneath a green baseball cap that is a dazzling canvas of pins and fishing lures and fake jewels. One pin quotes Chief Seattle: "The earth does not belong to us. We belong to the earth."

Emile hardly ever raises his eyes when he speaks. When he does, it is only to look at Ted Gordon. When he speaks to me, he looks down or out toward the horizon. But he speaks in a clipped stream of words, each bouncing out like those cranberries on the conveyor belt.

"Where you located?" he asks me but looks toward the black cat on the Dodge.

"Virginia Beach."

"How you get up here? I'd a stayed down there. You need a cat, dontcha? Take a couple. Take a coupla cats and put 'em in there. Take a couple." He points toward Gordon's jeep.

"No, I don't think so, Emile," Ted says. Ted begins to talk about the last time he saw Emile, hitchhiking into Chatsworth and then hitchhiking back a few hours later. Ted picked him up both ways.

"This is a slow lookin' road," Emile says, looking up and down the dirt path in front of his house. "Hell, you can't get no ride on this road." It seems as if Emile would like to have us stay, to tell a few more stories, to hear his laughter twang against the sound of other voices, but we don't linger because we're heading toward a ghost town in the area.

He watches us go and offers a toothless grin. His words snap against one another, syllables popping like caps, "If you got a cat in there, keep on going. If you got a cat in there, take it back to Virginia."

July 1, 1810: This month begins with moder-
ately cool weather. Furnace making iron fast.
Mick making feet for stoves. All hands at
their usual employment.

—Caleb Earle,
"The Martha Furnace Diary"

The first white men came to the Pine Barrens in the early 1700s. They were woodcutters and built sawmills. Next came the men who worked with iron, for in the stream beds was bog ore, and as John McPhee wrote, "Most of the now vanished towns in the pines were iron towns—small, precursive Pittsburghs, in every part of the forest, where five grades of pig and wrought iron were made." The furnaces in these towns produced thousands of cannonballs for the Continental Army during the Revolutionary War. They made wrought-iron fences, nails, ovens, and kettles. The metal was dug from the banks of the streams or beds of swamps. There were furnace towns and forge towns, little feudal estates where the muddy iron deposits were blasted and shaped. According to the Federal Writers' Project of the WPA in *Stories of New Jersey*, these towns were thriving places in the southern part of the state:

Sometimes as many as 600 people would be living in one of these communities close to the furnace or forge in the heart of the woods. The center of communal life was the master's (manager's) home, called the "big house," usually an elaborate establishment with a vegetable patch and flower garden. Here the workmen brought their problems and grievances, and the stranger could always find supper and a night's lodging. Schools, stores, churches, sawmills and gristmills were built for the workers and their families.

Ted Gordon leads me through Harrisville, a paper mill town that has vanished but for some crumbling foundations and even more subtle clues that only a scout obsessed with the past could find. Gordon is just such a scout. "If there's a trail out here that I haven't been on," he says, "then I'd like to know about it. It has to have been built in the last few months." At his home, Gordon has twenty-five filing cabinets filled with information on the Pines. He has over ten thousand slides on the area. "Fifty percent of the things I've photographed down here," he says, "no longer exist." He has been exploring the area for nearly half a century. Like McPhee, he got geological survey maps and roamed the trails. But Gordon, unlike McPhee, has made the area his life's work. "I know every sand trail from Monmouth to Cape May County."

We walk, like weary travelers in the early nineteenth century, down the old Tuckerton Stage Route, into what was once called Harrisville. Originally called McCartyville, the name of the town was changed when the Harris brothers bought the paper mill in the mid-1800s. The Harrises, like the McCartys, made paper from the salt hay they got from the marshes of the Jersey coast. In the 1880s Harrisville was a thriving little town with sandstone houses and a gristmill. The owner's home reportedly had a gold-plated piano in a room paneled in black walnut. At the heart of the town was the paper mill, three hundred feet long and two and a half stories high. Its stone walls were three feet thick and the basement of the main building had two thirteen-foot brick arches.

The path we walk along was once the straight line that ran through the town, edged by planted maples and gas lamps that stood like sentinels on iron posts. Harrisville was a modern town at the time, in the center of what was an industrial area. Farmers and iron workers did their shopping there. It was only a few miles to the furnaces at Speedwell, Martha, Batsto, or Atsion. Tuckerton, the third officially established port of entry in the United States, was only a short distance to the east with its customhouse and foreign trade. The town had its own gas plant, blacksmith's shop, a brick forge, and well-kept houses that the Harrises rented out to their workers. The Harrises ruled their community like feudal lords, demanding that each tenant keep paper and debris from the walkways and maintain neat front yards.

But just as the bog iron industry started to fade, the paper mills crumbled under the weight of frequent depressions and unwise management. By 1891 the Harris

Mill was sold at a sheriff's sale. By 1896 it had been sold again, and most of the residents had moved away. Within a few years the gas lamps and trimmed yards, the children calling to one another from back yards, the smoke from cookstoves, had all disappeared. In 1810 a fire destroyed what was left of the town, leaving what Ted Gordon and I saw on this crisp November morning—sandstone skeletons, shards of stone from the mills, declivities where homes once stood, and a pervasive, ghostly silence.

Gordon stops, kneels on the sandy road, picks up a flat stone, and draws a map of what the area would have looked like over a hundred years ago. He forms lines and squares to show a house or store, a group of rectangles to depict the old mill, a curving line to indicate the canal, a snaking cut to point out the Wading River. Still kneeling, he looks up as if he has heard a voice in the distance. "This was the most fashionable district in the Pines," he says. Somehow, he still seems to think it is, and as he gets up and walks over to a black walnut tree that has sprouted in a depression resembling the indentation from a meteor, he appears to see the people who were once here, who once slept confidently within these invisible walls.

Within a few minutes we are in Martha Furnace, examining pieces of slag iron that speckle the sandy road. Pitch pine cones, resinous and armed like triceratops, crunch underfoot. "You are walking on the bottom of the ocean here," Gordon tells me, and it is easy to believe him because there is nothing at the moment but a buzzing, watery silence. This seems ironic, since the iron mills were very noisy places, filled with constant activity. John McPhee describes them this way:

> The furnaces of the Pine Barrens were started up each year in the spring when the ice was gone and spillways from dammed streams again turned the waterwheels that powered giant bellows, which kept the furnaces in blast until winter froze them out. Men worked in twelve-hour shifts. There were no days off, and the happiest day of the year was the day the furnace went out of blast. In furnace towns, bog iron was crushed under great stamping hammers, and in the forge towns pig iron was worked into anconies of wrought iron under forge hammers that weighed more than five hundred pounds. Miles away, teamsters coming over the sand roads with loads of shells from the coast could hear the din through the forest, as could ore raisers out in the bogs, and colliers—as charcoal-makers were known in the pines—working at their pits.

The era of the bog iron industry in the Pine Barrens ended around the 1830s, around the time high-grade coal and iron ore were discovered in western Pennsylvania, but not even time and history can silence the imagination and the rhythmic pounding that seems now to come from the dark woods around us.

> *In 1936, a cousin of the fire watcher Eddie Parker was caught in the middle when a head fire and a backfire came together. He had no time to get to burned ground. The last living thing he did was to kneel, as he burned, and embrace a pine tree.*
>
> —John McPhee, *The Pine Barrens*

There are two principal places in the Pine Barrens where the trees grow to an average height of only five feet. These forests are filled with scrub oak, blackjack oak, and pitch pine. The shrubs are primarily black huckleberry and low bush blueberry. The early settlers made note of these dwarf forests, so scientists know that they have been around for at least a few hundred years, but they have never been able to come to perfect agreement on the causes of these pygmy trees. Some theorized about poor soil or toxic materials, others about wind conditions. But, finally, the only explanation that has been widely accepted is fire, which is regular and frequent on the Pine Plains.

From where I stand, on the crest of a hill overlooking the Upper Plains, it feels like Cape Cod without the ocean. The pines stretch out for miles, trees and plants undulating in a wave that varies in height from two feet to ten. It is an area where only the hardiest, most fire-resistant species can survive. Ted Gordon has seen many fires in the Pine Barrens. He has looked on as pitch pines have exploded, shooting balls of fiery tar across the highway and catching trees on the other side. "Fire," he says, "travels very fast here. And this landscape, which is one of my favorite places on earth, one of the natural wonders in this country, is a reminder that fire will always return."

From this vantage point 150 feet above sea level it seems as if the whole world stretches out before us, resilient, adaptive, in this fire-dominated landscape. There is only one way to get a better view in the Pine Barrens and that is from a fire tower. Apple Pie Hill Fire Tower is near Chatsworth, the town where we began our explorations. Back full circle, 268 feet higher than where we started, the Pine Barrens look newly made.

Jimmy Willett, a spry, sharp-eyed man in his early seventies with an Irish laughter and quick wit, is the fire observer. The lookout tower is about the size of a bathroom, and we stand around the azimuth circle, looking out through the twelve small panes of glass that make up the windows facing in each direction of the compass. Eight miles to the east is the spot where the Bear Swamp Hill Fire Tower used to stand. Now it's gone, and only Bear Swamp Hill stands with a notch cut into it, a bit to the right of its center, like a neat part in a schoolboy's head. In the early seventies, shortly after McPhee published his book with its opening description from the perspective of that location, a jet knocked over the tower and plowed through the top of the hill. To the south, on a crystal clear day, you can see the casinos in

Atlantic City. To the west, a new building with a copper tower in Philadelphia shines like a spotlight when the sun hits it just right. To the north is Arney's Mountain in Juliustown, near Fort Dix. There are blueberry fields to the left and right. The view extends, in oaks and pines, for seventeen miles.

On the tower, swaying gently in the breeze like a ship rolling in the ocean, I feel as if I am in the center of this strange world, separated from the outer urban circle and lifted above, just far enough so that the earth seems green and silent. Down below, though, at the foot of the tower is an old well meant for a sanitarium that a Dr. White from New York was planning to build many years ago. Like many projects in the Pine Barrens it started, then faded, and eventually disappeared . . . but not completely. In the old well is an overturned car, decaying leaves, and broken beer bottles, like pieces in an archaeological dig.

The previous evening, in Atsion, a town John McPhee described as "the country's only permanent non-existent land boom," I met Marion Burr, a ranger in the Wharton State Forest. A diminutive blonde, built wide and low to the ground, Burr talked with me about some of the oddities in the area. We talked about McPhee's depiction of the place as one of those instant paradises that never became a developer's Eden:

> In the eighteen-sixties, the name of Atsion was changed to Fruitland and the surrounding woods were divided

into small lots. Pamphlets titled "Cheap Lands, Homes for the Homeless, the Wild Lands of New Jersey" were handed out on New York City sidewalks. "The New Jersey wilderness shall be transformed into farms and fields of grain," the pamphlet said. "A large population should take the place of a few scattered families of wood-choppers and coal burners and their concomitants of ignorance, sin, and wretchedness. Let the forest be made flagrant with fruit blossoms!" In short time the name of Fruitland was changed back to Atsion, and the woods remained unflagrant.

Now, perhaps, they had become flagrant in a different manner. I told Burr that earlier when I was strolling around the Carranza monument, the memorial to Mexico's Lindbergh who crashed and died in the Pine Barrens, I found pornographic photographs strewn along one of the paths. She responded by touching the handle of the gun in her holster and saying, "There's a lot more out there than we'll ever know. There's so much space. Who knows who's gathering in these woods and for what purposes? Jimmy Hoffa may be out there. Who knows? We get it all out here—rapes, deviants, bodies."

Therefore, I'm not as surprised as I might have been when Ted Gordon turns back onto the main road and we pass a white stretch limousine, as long as a sixteen-wheeler it seems, or when I see through the rearview mirror that it has vanished like the angel of death onto one of those twisting sand roads snaking into a dark mouth of woods.

THE PRESENT

I have met Pine Barrens people who have, at one time or another, moved to other parts of the country. Most of them tried other lives for a while, only to return unreluctantly to the pines. One of them explained to me, "It's a privilege to live in these woods."

—John McPhee, *The Pine Barrens*

My parting conversation with Ted Gordon is about Bill Wasovwich, another important character in McPhee's story about the area. Wasovwich, now about fifty, is still living in the Pines, although no longer in Hog Wallow near Fred Brown's place. "He is still doing the same stuff he's always been doing," Gordon says, "pineballing, blueberrying, gathering sphagnum moss. He's one of those guys who makes up his mind to do something and he does it. It doesn't matter how long it takes. He just does it." Wasovwich works as a caretaker of a hunting lodge, a job which allows him to pick and choose his employments. In a variation on what McPhee called the three-part Piney repetition, Gordon says of Wasovwich: "He loves the woods. Really loves the woods. He's a real woodsman." I'm inclined to think the same could be said of Ted Gordon.

Shortly after I returned home from the Pine Barrens, I sent a copy of a story I had written about John McPhee to him. Three days later I received a call. I was happy to hear that he liked the story. He had read it carefully and made some notes. I was surprised that he would take the time to look over my work so meticulously. We spoke for about twenty minutes about points of fact and some issues of interpretation.

Toward the end of the conversation he mentioned my describing him as wearing corduroy pants, a faded green shirt, blue socks, and brown walking shoes. "By the way," he said, "I don't own any blue socks." I realized then that they must have been black, and I knew that for a craftsman like McPhee even the smallest detail was part of the finished work, that everything had to be painstakingly fitted together with a steady hand, guided by a sure eye. In a December 28, 1992, issue of *The New Yorker*, McPhee describes his relationship with the recently deceased editor William Shawn:

He understood the disjunct kinship of creative work— every kind of creative work—and time. The most concise summation of it I've ever heard was seven words he said just before closing my first Profile and sending it off to press. It was 1965, and I was a new young writer, and he did not entrust new writers to any extent whatever to other editors. He got the new ones started by himself. So there we were—hours at a session—discussing reverse pivots and backdoor plays and the role of the left-handed comma in the architectonics of basketball while *The New Yorker* hurtled toward its deadlines. I finally had to ask him, "How can you afford to use so much time and go into so many things in such detail when this whole enterprise is yours to keep together?"

He said, "It takes as long as it takes."

As a part-time writing teacher, I have offered those words to a generation of students. If they are writers, they will never forget them.

This description of Shawn could serve as well to describe McPhee—and perhaps, in a certain respect, Ted Gordon, too. Ted Gordon, former high school teacher of German, amateur botanist, and woodsman, had the same obsession for the smallest truth, the same fascination with all aspects of the woods. Both McPhee and Gordon shuttled back and forth, it seemed, between their respective monks' cells and the world, reflective and involved. Both, like Browning's Fra Lippo Lippi, seemed to believe: "This world's no blot for us, / Nor blank; it means intensely, and means good." As I thought of them, another idea came into my mind, and I looked down, wondering what color socks I was wearing or if I was even wearing any at all.

CHAPTER 6

ENGLAND /
IRELAND

We are such stuff
As dreams are made on, and our little life
Is rounded with a sleep.
> —William Shakespeare, *The Tempest*

I must lie down where all the ladders start,
In the foul rag-and-bone shop of the heart.
> —William Butler Yeats,
> "The Circus Animals' Desertion"

And with that word we riden forth our weye.
> —Geoffrey Chaucer,
> *The Canterbury Tales*

Ho, talk saves us.
> —James Joyce, *Finnegans Wake*

I was in my late twenties the first time I saw my grandfather. He had been dead for nearly fifty years. I had imagined him often but never as he appeared in that photograph, which seemed to have been scalded white by time. A relative had discovered the picture and sent it to me, and I studied it as if it were my own face I was examining.

He was probably in his late thirties. His light brown hair was thick and cut short, shaved close at the sides and waxed back into a crewcut in the front. His generous moustache hung profusely over his lower lip and curled stiffly into an elegant handlebar. His nose inclined down to an aristocratic point, and his right eyebrow arched just enough to suggest a Prussian pride. His suit was formal, and he wore a white bow tie that was barely visible against the stiff white collar. But it was his eyes that drew me into the frame. The black-and-white photograph did not tell me the color but my guess was blue, like mine and those of my sons. His gaze was direct and deep, as if he were looking at something over my right shoulder, as if he saw his future, my past, there beyond the camera lens.

His name was Ottomar, but he was more handsome, less rigid, I supposed, than his name suggested. He had been born in the autumn of 1845 in Halle-on-the-Sal, Germany. By the time my father was born, he was sixty-eight years old. He died when he was eighty-seven. In between he had lived a life: two wives, two families, two countries. Two of his brothers fought for

Prussia in the Franco-Prussian War in 1870, but he came to the United States and settled in Brooklyn, leaving much that he loved behind. His own father, whom I had once glimpsed in an old portrait, had looked like a Nantucket sea captain with a white beard, wind-swept hair, and watery blue eyes, but he had been a professor in a German university. When Ottomar came to America, he brought his father's portrait among his few belongings.

After his first wife died and his children were grown, he married Katie Kolb, who had been born in Paris and raised in the Alsace-Lorraine; she had traveled to America by herself as a teenager and worked as a maid. She was twenty-eight years his junior. Together they had six children whom they raised in the Ridgewood section of New York City. Otto, as he was called, made riding habits and fine clothes for the mayor and other wealthy residents of the city.

Looking at the photograph, at those eyes that seemed to yearn for great distances, I often imagined his life. I saw him in the market square of Halle, angling among the stalls, stealing an apple, and disappearing into the side streets. I pictured him preparing to leave his country forever. I thought of him as a tailor, a man who loved his craft. Perhaps, like Gay Talese's father, he had that "mild mental disorder that is endemic to the tailoring trade." In *Unto the Sons* Talese describes the occupation in ways that seemed to me to match my grandfather's meditative look: "A tailor's eye must follow a seam precisely, but his pattern of thought is free to veer off in different directions, to delve into his life, to ponder his past, to lament lost opportunities, create dramas, imagine slights, brood, exaggerate—in simple terms, the tailor when sewing has too much time to think." My grandfather's deep and distant gaze might have been directed, I thought, into eternity or toward some other fathomless place.

But I had only dreams to feed my speculations. There were not more than a few basic facts and some snapshots to go on. With my mother's family it was much the same—a few photographs, a vague lineage that traced its way back to Ireland, both North and South, Hunters and Findlans. Gazing out the darkening windows of the plane as we floated miles above the Atlantic Ocean heading toward Europe, I realized that my idle thoughts about grandfathers and grandmothers were simply a desire to recollect stories. Growing up, I had breathed in stories from Ireland and England. My past came from the stories in Shakespeare and Yeats and Dickens and Hardy. It seemed natural enough, then, as I headed toward England for the first time, to feel as if I were going home, to hear familiar voices.

The morning broke in on us with a sudden clarity. The clouds below were a snowy plateau broken only occasionally by a fissure of blue sky and water. Then Ireland, like a Druidical shadow, slid into view. By nine in the morning my eyes were on fire from lack of sleep, and I felt lightheaded from the beginnings of jet lag, but I was awake enough to notice the shadow of the plane skim across a rainbow as we descended into a soupy fog and then came within view of the neatly parceled English countryside.

The island that stretched before me was about three times the size of Virginia, but it seemed as big as another planet. When I was a boy the narrative of England floated through many of my afternoons in school—a land of kings and conquests, bloody battles, Plantagenets and Tudors. But more than a story of conquests, it was a tale of enslavement that came to life in history class in the stories told by the thin-lipped Marist Brother who described the rocky jut of land that drifted off the edge of the European continent when the sea level rose after the Ice Age. He described the hunters crossing the land bridge and later the Celts invading the British Isles as they had overrun most of Western Europe. They conquered the natives and absorbed the cultures with their priests, the Druids, dominating the society. Then came Roman rule and soon after the influence of Christianity. By 600 the Angles and Saxons possessed England, and perhaps this is when England's true history begins, with those tribes in the fifth century who called it "Angle-Land." In the ninth century Alfred the Great unified the country, creating laws and governmental structures. In 1066, with the Norman invasion, Anglo-Saxon rule ended and within a century the modern dynasties began.

THE PRESENT

But I found the real England in my junior literature class at Mount St. Michael High School. In that class I discovered the England of *Beowulf* and *Sir Gawain and the Green Knight*, the England of Wordsworth and Shelley and Keats, a landscape of sweet music, sad stories, and early death. Even our teacher had an insouciant manner, an ironic smile, and a wan angularity—the look, I supposed, of a Romantic poet. The stories about Shelley and Byron poured from him and washed over me like waves that slowly but inevitably change the shoreline. Listening to him then I knew that one day I would travel through Stratford and London and Ireland, listening to the people and seeing where the stories grew. I would not have guessed, however, that it would take twenty-five years to feel the comforting skid of the plane's wheels on English soil. Nor would I have imagined some of the strange turns the journey would take.

The best laid schemes . . .
                    —Robert Burns, "To a Mouse"

Soon after reaching our hotel in London our bags were lost. My wife looked at me with eyes that seemed to sense the future, and I remembered with a certain irony the red-cheeked customs clerk who said to me enviously, "Drink the Guinness in Ireland. There's nothing like it in the world. I wish I were in your boat." But it wasn't long before the seas got rough. Eventually our bags were found, but the confusion appeared to fore-shadow the future. Our bags were lost again when we flew back from Ireland ten days later. But before that we were robbed on the train between London and Hollyhead, where we were to take the ferry. My jacket was stolen with my wallet and credit cards and traveler's checks. If it hadn't been for a kindly older English-woman who bore a striking resemblance to Dame May Whitty in Alfred Hitchcock's *The Lady Vanishes* and who convinced us to take a gift of twenty pounds, we would not have had enough cash to pay for the insurance on the car rental in Dun Laoghaire. On our way from Dun Laoghaire to Dublin, where we were sent to find an American Express teller machine somewhere in the surreal crowds and darkening shadows of Upper O'Connell Street, our car broke down in the middle of a major intersection. I pushed it through the pouring rain. But even pushing, I found out, was easier than driving on Ireland's country paths in the dark, on the left side, as cars whizzed along roads too narrow, it seemed, even for a bicycle. By the next day I had learned how to negotiate those roads. I had even acquired a taste for stout. And when Delta Airlines called just as we had stepped out the door of the farmhouse where we were staying four days later in Cleggan, along the rocky coast of Western Ireland, saying that all flights to America were cancelled that afternoon, I needed a drink. We had no money left, our credit cards were gone, and the rental car was due back at the airport. Two days later, after a flight on a Russian jet, another experience with lost luggage, and thirteen hours in Dulles Airport, we made it home to find one son waiting for us at the Norfolk airport while the other two slept on the living room couch and in bed, oblivious to the pizza cartons, dishes, and dirty socks strewn around the rooms.

But even though fate obviously had its own plans for us, we stumbled along the route we had decided upon. The first woman I met on the train from London to Canterbury turned out to be an English exile living in Atlanta and visiting her aged mother. The woman had long dark hair, frizzled by rain and wind, bright eyes, and a face lined like a New Mexican arroyo. "I'll tell you what to look for," she told me, "lace curtains. Every house has lace curtains. Most are white, once in a while you'll see yellow ones. Some even have different shapes—those are the areas that don't conform. Each time I come back I think perhaps the curtains will be gone, that the people will have risen up and—I don't know—put up shades or something. That's why I left England as a young girl, I think, lace curtains. I couldn't take all those lace curtains, all that conformity, the class consciousness. Even the American South will accept the nouveau riche. Not here. I was from the working class, and that's where I was expected to stay." I didn't bother to mention John Major's rude beginnings but instead sat back into the silence punctuated by the clacking of the train. There were only twenty-five pilgrims in our car going to Canterbury, but they appeared to be a good cross-section of modern England, as Chaucer's were of the medieval times. Child and adult, black and white, bird watcher and Bible reader, the elegant and the shabby all sat in a pleasant, wakeful quiet. It was a sooty day, and the outlying towns seemed silenced by the grayness. The train slowed as we passed a row of attached houses, and I caught a glimpse of a moon-eyed young woman with a faraway look, her face flickering like a candle in the opening in the lace curtains. We clattered along past soccer fields and parks, paint stores and blanketed horses, black birds and townhouses, stacks of hay, rolling hills, sand pits, used bookstores, stony fields, cemeteries, and apple orchards. The pilgrims on the train, unlike Chaucer's, remained reserved, meditative. Our journey, however, was done in ninety minutes, and Chaucer's pilgrims never finished theirs. But Chaucer told enough of the story to interest six hundred years' worth of readers.

Other than the record of his career as a courtier and civil servant, little is known of Geoffrey Chaucer's life. His father was a successful London wine merchant and Geoffrey was most likely educated at the Latin grammar school of St. Paul's Cathedral. He was a page to the Countess of Ulster, a squire to Edward III, and eventually a servant to John of Gaunt, the Duke of Lancaster. He worked as a comptroller of customs in London and a clerk of the king's works. He was a soldier, a representative to Parliament, a justice of the peace, and a diplomat. But, despite all his business and political successes, what he is remembered for is his dazzling collection of stories, *The Canterbury Tales*, which recounts the journey of a group of pilgrims from Southwark, just outside of London, to Canterbury Cathedral, the shrine of St. Thomas à Becket. It was probably in 1386, when he was pushed out of his political offices because his patron John of Gaunt left England on an expedition and the Duke of Gloucester began to influence young King Richard II, that Chaucer began to compose and organize *The Canterbury Tales*. It was an immense project—thirty pilgrims telling four stories each. But Chaucer completed only twenty-five of the projected one hundred and twenty tales. Nevertheless, what he did complete was a supreme achievement, a portrait of an entire nation, a microcosm of fourteenth-century English society, from plowman to knight, a picture of young and old, men and women, scholar and seducer. Each tale suits the teller.

When I first read Chaucer in high school, the tales that suited me the most were the ribald ones featuring hot pokers and mock floods, the jokes about excrement, the stories of skittish but willing maidens and lecherous students. It reminded me of life in the Bronx, partly as it was but mostly as I wished it to be.

We arrived at Canterbury Cathedral that Sunday in time to attend Mass. First built when St. Augustine brought Christianity to the country, Canterbury is the mother church of England. The current Dean of Canterbury described the spiritual power of the place when he said, "At the site of the martyrdom of Thomas Becket and in the Chapel of Twentieth Century Martyrs, men and women are confronted with the cost of Christian faith." When we arrived, the Bishop of Dover, a ruddy-cheeked, white-haired man in his late fifties, was giving a robust sermon: "Noah and I have something in common. We both built boats. But that's where the similarity ends. His was a gigantic ark; mine was a sixteen-foot dinghy. And mine sunk."

He described his boat capsizing, the woman who saved him from the frigid waters, his relief. The story of Noah, he pointed out, was also a story of rescue. His voice rose a notch: "Our society is aware that something is dreadfully awry and out of sorts. Do not doubt it—you and I are not simply off course. We have capsized . . . perhaps we did not start the war in Bosnia, but we each add to the sum of the world's sadness. There are not only causes but there are reasons. And you and I are part of the reason. As for Noah, so for us. God has absolutely practical things for us to do. . . . It is God who made you, and He hasn't finished with you yet."

I still had my wallet at this point; therefore, I probably didn't take his message fully to heart, but I paid careful attention to the confirmation ceremony he performed: "Do you turn to Christ? Do you repent your sins? Do you renounce evil?"

Stern tones from the bishop and choral answers from the young men and women. Candle flames danced in the drafts, and the sunlight was threaded with purple and red as it came through the stained-glass windows. The bishop called for a moment of silent prayer for those to be confirmed, but my thoughts carried me back to my own confirmation in the fifth grade at St. Philip Neri Church, which was far less majestic than Canterbury Cathedral, but in our red robes, waiting for the slap of the bishop and his words which would tell us we were soldiers of Christ, we certainly felt much the same as these young people—inspired by the ritual but eager to disrobe and resume our old, unchanged lives. Our names were different—Murray, Fitzpatrick, DeCaprio, Esposito—but Munday and Withrington and Perrin looked as ready to reach the sunlight as we once were.

I stayed to watch six bird-beaked deacons finish off the bread and wine from the Eucharist and then to walk through the still church, past tombs and effigies. There was no onion-stone here but rather monuments worthy of bishops and princes dead these six hundred years and more—John Stratford, Edward Plantagenet, and others. As we left Canterbury we passed two homeless men selling bunches of "hand-picked" daffodils before the gates to the cathedral, and on the train back to London, we sat next to three young men, bedecked in strafed denim and black leather, their feet up on the seats across from them, having a conversation the Bishop of Dover might have understood well: "We've been on this train a long fuckin' time, eh? Where'd all these fuckin' people come from?"

England/Ireland

The next morning the sky was pale blue and the air smelled of heather and English tea as the train passed hedge-framed fields and hillsides dotted with sheep on the route to Stratford-upon-Avon. The town is not easy to get to without a car. By train it requires a few changes, the final one on a spur line that seems worn and rusting. But, perhaps, it all adds to the mystery surrounding Shakespeare's life.

In a letter to a friend a few years before he died John Keats said, "A man's life of any worth is a continual allegory—and very few eyes can see the mystery of his [Shakespeare's] life. . . . Shakespeare led a life of allegory: his works are the comments on it." Shakespeare's life will probably always be a tantalizing mystery, an elliptical allegory, about which only a few facts are available, and many of those are still ambiguous after all the scholarly probing. Much will never be known. That leaves the plays and poems to provide the best comment we will ever have on his life. In his plays we may find, as John Dryden did over three hundred years ago, "the man who of all modern and perhaps ancient poets had the largest and most comprehensive soul."

However, what we do know of the Bard's life is interesting and is just enough to tease us into imagining more. As Dennis Kay says in his recent biography of Shakespeare, "The Shakespeare family history is a textbook case of that upward social mobility that was so common in Renaissance England." Shakespeare, the third of eight children and the oldest son of John Shake-speare of Stratford-upon-Avon, was born, most histo-rians agree, on April 23, 1564. His father, a glover, was a prominent merchant, but the world William Shake-speare entered in 1564 was a harsh place: one out of every six people in Stratford died that year from the plague.

Shakespeare not only survived the plague, but he lived more than twenty years beyond the average Eliza-bethan life expectancy of just over thirty, becoming the greatest playwright of all time. Genius seems independ-ent of environmental determinants, but Shakespeare did not rise fully formed like Athena from Zeus's head. He went to school in Stratford, learning besides Latin grammar and composition something about drama. Education in Stratford was influenced by the renowned British pedagogue Richard Mulcaster, who stressed elo-quence, performance and originality. Clearly, Shake-speare was a quick study.

However, during Elizabethan times there was no adolescence for any but the aristocracy. Only one out of the twenty-six males christened in Stratford in 1564 went on with a full-time education. In the late 1570s Shakespeare left school, thereby leaving little trail for his future biographers to follow. He may have trav-eled, worked as a schoolmaster, been a soldier or law-yer, studied to be an actor, or engaged in heavy bouts of drinking. Whatever course he followed, in 1582 when he was eighteen, a minor who needed his father's approval, he married Anne Hathaway, twenty-six and pregnant.

Shakespeare may have felt trapped, as Dennis Kay speculates, realizing "that his youthful folly with a woman already moving rapidly out of the marriageable range was something for which he was conscious of having to pay, and pay dearly." Perhaps, but the facts are that he fathered three children—Susanna in 1583 and the twins Hamnet and Judith in 1585—and shortly after left on a hundred-mile journey to London to seek his fortune as an actor and playwright. Legend has it that he left Stratford after he was caught poaching one of Sir Thomas Lucy's deer, but whether he was escaping the scene of a crime or a lackluster marriage will remain a mystery. It is clear, though, that he began writing, making his work the city's play, as Dennis Kay put it. It must have been a daring adventure for a man in his early twenties to enter the riot of commercial life in London, 150,000 people—tailors and merchants, pickpockets and prostitutes all swapping services—and look to conquer the city with his imagination. Eventually, he conquered far more than London.

Shakespeare will always be a mysterious figure suspended in our dreams between Stratford and London, between the city and the country. In his will he left his wife his "second best bed," which could be a sign of affection or a slight. He was a passionate artist but a man who in the last weeks of his life was more concerned with his family's well-being than his own claim to immortality. He was a writer who inspired his contemporary and fellow dramatist Ben Jonson to say, "He was indeed honest, and of an open, and free nature: had an excellent Fancy; brave notions, and gentle expressions." He was a father whose son Hamnet died at twelve years old, but he was a man who left no record in letter or speech about his sorrow. The record he left is in the plays. In them is the allegory of his life. In them can be found all the sadness and joy, the generous spirit, the anger, the dark introspection. The mystery that is the man can be discovered most profoundly there. As I entered Stratford, I couldn't help imagining the overwhelming despair he must have felt in 1596 when his son died and wondering if a few years later in *Hamlet* he was perhaps not thinking of his child when he wrote: " . . . this goodly frame, the earth, seems to me a sterile promontory; this most excellent canopy, the air, look you, this brave o'erhanging firmament, this majestical roof fretted with golden fire, why, it appears no other thing to me than a foul and pestilent congregation of vapours."

As we approached Stratford, angling past the city dump, Toyota and Renault dealerships, and electrical contractors, things didn't seem very promising. There are no Shakespeares left in the town, but the phone book still lists the name: Shakespeare Country Chem-Dry, Shakespeare Fish Bar, the Shakespeare Hotel, the Shakespeare Rest Home, a few inns, a taxi company, a wine store, and a center for people with physical disabilities. But it turned out to be a lovely English village. To get to Shakespeare's birthplace I had one more obstacle course, however, through the Minories Shopping Mall (Trendy Toys, Laura Ashley, March Hare, Daydreams, Aquasail—the snow and surf shop). Finally I stood next to the bed in the room where Shakespeare was most likely born, a bed that appeared to be less than five and a half feet long. As I stood there imagining the Bard dangling his legs over the edge or raising his five-foot-two-inch frame off the bed as the sun rose, a conversation between a young woman and one of the guides broke into my daydreams.

"I've devoted my life to Shakespeare," the young woman told the guide.

"I see."

"I *know* Shakespeare. And I don't believe the theory that he wrote all the plays. That's only one person's *theory*. There's lots of proof that the plays were written by many different people."

"Ah, I see."

"I've studied this extensively. Shakespeare was just an ordinary man."

On my way to the New Place, the house that Shakespeare bought after his more-than-ordinary success in the London theater, I stopped in the Stratford Library to take a closer look at an advertisement on the bulletin board, an ad the groundlings might have enjoyed:

Wanted!
. . . Preferably Alive
Chubby Ladies

It was an advertisement for an exercise class in the town, but somehow it was difficult to envision a group of overweight maidens bouncing to "Staying Alive" in the vicinity. It would have been as easy to imagine a bingo game in Canterbury Cathedral.

It was a chubby lady, though, who opened the door and greeted us at the New Place, the home Shakespeare paid 120 pounds for a few years before he died. The second most expensive house in Stratford at the time, the remaining foundation suggests its grandeur. Nearby is the Nash house, where Shakespeare's daughter Susanna and her husband Dr. John Hall lived. Hall was a doctor, a prescriber of medicines, not one of the surgeon-barbers who also worked during the times. Barbers acted as surgeons, it seems, because they were the ones who had access to sharpened instruments. The same man who cut your hair and trimmed your beard also amputated your limbs if necessary, and sometimes if not. Even Hall, although not prone to use such drastic measures, left behind a diary that recounts his striking prescriptions: "A child of Mr. Walkers of Imington, minister, aged six months, afflicted with the falling-sickness, by consent was thus freed. First, I caused pieces of peony-root to be hanged about the neck; when the fit afflicted I commanded to be applied with a sponge to the nostrils the juice of rue mixed with white wine vinegar . . . the hair was powdered with the roots of peony. . . . Thus the child was delivered from all its fits." A mild sort of torture that probably would get any child to stand up straight, and surely better than amputation.

I stood in the Hall house, dreamily gazing out the window toward the garden, thinking about the doctor's innocent patients when a flash of gold by the heavy-limbed mulberry tree in the yard caught my eye. It was my wife's hair in the sunlight, flashing exactly as it had twenty years before when we had recited our wedding vows, quoting Shakespeare's sonnet 116 which described love as "an ever-fixed mark / That looks on tempests and is never shaken. . . . Love alters not with his brief hours and weeks, / But bears it out even to the edge of doom." Luckily for me, Shakespeare seemed to have spoken truly.

On our way back to London we stopped briefly in Oxford as a smoky purple mist mixed with the darkening sky. There were more bicycles and more stunning architecture than I had ever seen in one place. A professor from Canada led us into the town, saying, "It's not the real world, but who needs the real world?" The university has been called the "city of dreaming spires." It is the oldest university in the country, dating back to Saxon times. Keats called it "the finest city in the world," and Hawthorne said, "There's no other place like it in the world, it is a despair to see such a place and ever to leave it." We had only two hours, like a blink of our eyes in the darkness, a night dream of chapels and quadrangles, book shops and winding streets, rolling rivers, parks, and meadows. I understood what Hawthorne meant.

We took the tube back from Paddington Station to the center of the city. Unlike Oxford, this *was* the real world. Like the New York City subways, this was the grimy real thing—weary bobbing heads, glazed eyes, silent gloominess. And the ads were reminiscent of New York, with perhaps two differences. One ad read: "Bombs—be alert. If you see an unattended package or bag in this car, do not touch it. Move away. . . . Tell the driver or the underground staff. . . . Tell the other passengers to leave the area. . . . Never ignore it." Another offered a quotation from T. S. Eliot's "Prelude": "The winter evening settles down . . ." The two ads seemed strikingly un-American, but somehow appropriate for the "underground," offering bomb threats and Eliot, a narrow hope indeed.

The next morning we decided to do our tourist duty and observe the changing of the guard and visit the Tower of London. We refused to be daunted by a group of articles that appeared in *The (London) Times* that morning—"Fire expert uncovers catalogue of danger at Hampton Court," "Tourists in Tower step up to danger," and "Top tourist sites condemned as dated and dull." We watched the changing of the guard, although I'll remember some acquaintances I made among the crowd more than I will the pomp and ceremony. The Tower was a different story, a gruesome one told with wonderful skill and dark humor by the Beefeater, or yeoman warder, guide. Helen Hanff in *Q's Legacy* said, "I was glad we didn't line up to see the Crown Jewels; it would have been like seeing the Taj Mahal and Auschwitz on the same day." We did see both, and the jewels were certainly impressive, but the Tower was memorable, for it seemed to me to sum up the bloody drama, the high comedy, the history, the interlocking stories that for me were England. The guide offered a steady stream of tales about heads impaled upon spikes; jokes about executioners, bags of coins, and severance pay; stories of Thomas More and the Bell Tower; descriptions of the two-ton portcullis; and anecdotes about Sir Walter Raleigh's thirteen-year imprisonment. He described executions in graphic detail, telling us about the executioner who was a part-time butcher and full-time drunkard who delivered five strokes of the ax but was still unable to sever his victim's head. Sinew and bone held it until the red-eyed butcher retrieved one of his knives to finish the task. Two ravens, their wings clipped to keep them earthbound, sat near the base of one of the towers as the guide intoned about the rack and screams of agony, boys being smothered, wives poisoned, and prisoners cheating fate by drinking themselves to death.

THE PRESENT

The Tower had become a theater of sorts; it seemed appropriate enough, then, to head from there to a play. The cab drove past a group of Dickensian young men with torn shirts and tangled hair; near Westminster Abbey, where Chaucer and other English writers are buried; and along the South Bank of the Thames by the site of Shakespeare's Globe. It was an area known as Bear Gardens, which during Shakespeare's times was famous for bear-baiting, a form of Elizabethan entertainment that drew larger crowds than the Bard's tragedies. In such amusements the bear would be tied to a stake in the center of a ring, and a group of large dogs would be set upon it. Mutilated dogs were replaced by fresh ones. When the bear was brought down or killed, a new one was brought forward. Sometimes, for the sake of variety, there would be a blinded bear or a horse running free in the ring with an ape on its back set on by the dogs.

The play we had tickets for, *Burbage and the Bard*, was an inventive account of the life of Shakespeare seen through the eyes of his friend, the actor Richard Burbage, and was showing at the Lilian Baylis Theater, on a street that gave even knowledgeable London taxi drivers moment's pause. But after a few wrong turns we found it, a small theater but with plenty of room for the fifteen of us who sat in the audience. As the driver pulled away from the curb he said, "Enjoy yourselves, mates, this is off, off, off Broadway."

We did enjoy ourselves. The play was a fascinating

blend of history, conjecture, and fiction interwoven with speeches from Shakespeare's plays. At one point, Burbage looked at Shakespeare, as he raked his index finger across his throat, and warned him, "If you parody the court figures, Will, we'll all end up in the Tower." Shakespeare never did end up in the Tower, and after my afternoon's visit to that place I understood why some of his plays were veiled so that the Lord Chamberlain's men never had to make the trip through Traitor's Gate.

The next morning, on our way to Euston Station to catch the train to get the ferry from Hollyhead to Ireland, we passed the University of London. Describing the place, our driver said, "They specialize in the sciences here. And you don't have to have that accent you do at Oxford, what? You know, sounding like you swallowed something awful." He paused to laugh at his own joke, then continued, "Oxford is the place you go to sleep for three or four years. It's for dreamers. We're more practical here in London."

I probably should have listened more carefully to him, but I suppose I'm like one of those dreamers he described because we were not more than an hour out of London when I discovered my jacket and wallet had been lifted without my even noticing. I might have been too engrossed in the current *Time* cover story on England, "Isle of Despair," even to see that this blessed plot, this earth, this realm, this England had actually had, as the magazine pointed out, "The longest recession since World War II . . . dragged on for 2½ chilling years, with no end in sight." My guard was down—after all I was far from New York City—as I rode through the picturesque English countryside. Perhaps my wallet was being stolen as I read, "Though murder and mayhem in Britain are still far below America's level, by one measure its crimes against property have exceeded the U.S. rate. Legions of permanently jobless big-city youths dwell in a subculture of vandalism and drugs, with no scruple about stealing several times a day."

> *I took more yarns into my head than prayers.*
> —Mickey Ward speaking to
> Lawrence Millman in
> *Our Like Will Not Be There Again*

After we had searched the train, talked to the police, and bemoaned our bad luck, there was nothing to do but get on the ferry to Ireland. The cold day had turned grayer than before and the Irish Sea resembled Buck Mulligan's in *Ulysses*, snot green and scrotumtightening. But after an hour of gentle rolling the sea turned the color of F. Scott Fitzgerald's eyes, and my thoughts turned to dreams of stories and to the two most famous of Irish storytellers.

William Butler Yeats's decision to become a writer did

not shock his family. His father, John Butler Yeats, had paved the way by taking an odd route. First, he went to Trinity College in Dublin intending to become a minister like his father and grandfather, but he turned to the law when he found no calling in the church. He passed the bar in 1866, the year after his son William was born, but his soul was no more in the law than it had been in the ministry. He was bored by the legal system and found himself drawing satirical sketches of court officials. According to Oscar Wilde, John Butler one morning at breakfast announced to his family that he was discarding his career as a lawyer to become a painter. In his biography of Oscar Wilde, Richard Ellmann recounts a typically Wildean interpretation of the scene: "To the question 'Could he paint?' Wilde would reply, 'Not in the least, that was the beauty of it.'" Perhaps Wilde told the story accurately, for the elder Yeats never made much of a success with his art. When he was sixty-eight years old, in 1907, he left Ireland to live in New York City, and he never returned to the country of his birth. According to Denis Donoghue, someone in Dublin described the adventure as the story of "an old man who ran away from home and made good," a Rip Van Winkle from the Old Sod.

Initially, William Butler Yeats wanted to be a painter, but art school helped him decide to be a poet instead. Like his father, he made not much more than a precarious living from his art. As Yeats said in *Dramatis Personae*, until he was nearly fifty he never made more than two hundred pounds per year from writing, but patrons like Lady Gregory recognized his genius and with help from her and others he was able "through the greater part of my working life to write without thought of anything but the beauty or the utility of what I wrote." And, of course, unlike his father, Yeats became a great success. In 1923 he won the Nobel Prize and lived the last sixteen years of his life with fortune, fame, and his talent intact.

From his love of Ireland and his spiritual marriage with Maud Gonne, the woman he proposed to many times but who refused each offer, he created the idea of the artist's "mask," the other self. He was always fascinated with contradictions, and from the most personal ones he made great poetry. As he once said, "We make out of the quarrel with others, rhetoric, but out of the quarrel with ourselves, poetry . . . we sing amid an uncertainty; and, smitten even in the presence of the most high beauty by the knowledge of our solitude, our rhythm shudders."

Of his disenchantment with the course of Irish nationalism he drew a picture of a greasy till and shivering prayer, saying that it seemed the modern Irish were "born to pray and save," for "Romantic Ireland's dead and gone, / It's with O'Leary in the grave." Of his unrequited love for the beautiful revolutionary Maud Gonne, he framed a modern Helen of Troy. His vision was of human history at once repetitious and progressive, a series of gyres or cycles that moved ever upward but along the same pattern. In his art he envisioned Byzantium, and a golden bird, singing of "what is past, or passing, or to come." But he knew always that the source of the imagination was in the "sweepings of the street," in experience. He is Ireland's greatest poet as Joyce is its greatest novelist. Between the two, they bring to life the country and the city, Western Ireland and Dublin, "the deep heart's core" and "the centre of paralysis."

James Joyce's father, like Yeats's, was unsuccessful, only much more dramatically so. Perhaps he epitomized what Oscar Wilde meant when he said, "We Irish are too poetical to be poets; we are a nation of brilliant failures." In *Portrait of the Artist as a Young Man*, Stephen Dedalus describes his father as a man who had been a medical student, an oarsman, a tenor, an amateur actor, a shouting politician, a small investor, a drinker, a good fellow, something in a distillery, a tax gatherer, a bankrupt, a storyteller, and a praiser of his own past. This may not definitively sum up the resume of John Stanislaus Joyce, but it comes close. As Robert M. Adams said of the writer: "He wrote no imaginative prose which was not deeply rooted in specific fact and experience." Joyce was an autobiographical writer, and in *Portrait of the Artist as a Young Man* he captured the essence of his father, whose main occupations were, according to Adams, "drink, recriminations, sponging, and sentimental talk." In a few years John Joyce, through drink and bad judgment, took his family from a respectable suburb to North Richmond Street, near the Dublin slums. "Within a decade," Adams says, "the family moved from comfort to squalor, without, however, abandoning its meager pretensions to a sort of connection with aristocracy."

Like his father, Joyce dabbled in a few careers before he found his way as a writer. He tried medical school for a short time, studied voice, and even entered a national competition for solo tenors. But he was destined to be a writer, and for him that meant being an expatriate. Ireland and its people were always his subjects, but he needed distance to see his "priest-ridden" country clearly. With Nora Barnacle, whom he had known for only four months but with whom he would live for the next thirty-seven years, Joyce took a midnight boat to the continent, and except for a trip home to visit his dying mother or a short stay in Dublin to become the manager of a movie house, he spent the rest of his life as an exile. No matter what the cost he was always the uncompromising artist without a country. From *Dubliners* to *Portrait of the Artist as a Young Man* to *Ulysses* and *Finnegans Wake*, he penetrated deeper into the heart of Dublin and its people than anyone before or since, seemingly unconcerned about whether his readers would or could follow his genius. He was unyielding with his talent and his expectations. *Finnegans Wake* took sixteen years to write, and rumor has it that Joyce expected readers to spend an equal amount of time reading and appreciating it. Whether this is true or not, Robert Adams makes it clear that the virtually blind Joyce struggled mightily to compose his complex epic: "Sizable portions of *Finnegans Wake* were written in a darkened room, where Joyce scrawled with a thick crayon single words on big sheets of yellow paper; over the last twenty years of his life, he was never far from blindness, and the psychological strain alone was evidently horrible." In *Dubliners* the recurrent theme is entrapment. The characters are victims of family, church, school, their friends, their own romantic delusions. Through writing Joyce strove to break the chains and, even though he understood the romantic irony of Stephen Dedalus's aims, to forge the uncreated conscience of his race.

By the time we reached Dun Laoghaire, it was dark and drizzling. Driving into Dublin as the rain became harder and the darkness blacker, I felt as if I were Bloom in Hades, isolated and lost. Years before I had been lost in the passage in *Ulysses* that began: "Now who is that lankylooking galoot over there in the macintosh? Now who is he I'd like to know? Now, I'd give a trifle to know who he is. Always someone turns up you never dreamt of. A fellow could live on his lonesome all his life." I never did figure out who Mackintosh was or who was wearing one, and for a time I thought I'd be just as lost among the lights and crowds of Dublin. People drove with what seemed to me a mad abandon, and I thought maybe Freud was right when he said that the Irish were the only race that could not profit from psychoanalysis. He was probably referring to their instinct for storytelling but to me their driving demonstrated a willing acceptance of death. Under different circumstances I think I would have loved the city, its shouts and drunken smiles, its swelling crowds and various hues, but it seemed surreal to me as I searched desperately for the American Express teller machine on Upper O'Connell Street. Even as I searched, though, I realized that my perspective was distorted by fatigue and depression, and at a different moment I would have agreed with Susan and Thomas Cahill: "Dublin should first be visited by night. In early morning, when the air is heavy with white smog from thousands of chimney pots and the sky is overcast, Dubliners are silent, white-faced people, who greet the day begrudgingly and often belatedly. Toward evening the rhythm of the city quickens, the noise level rises, and faces flush."

Joyce said that Dublin was the "centre of paralysis," but the phrase seemed to describe me, not the pulsating, lively city I found myself in and, once I had my traveler's checks replaced, I escaped immediately to a farmhouse in Prosperous, about nineteen miles to the west. The farming community was aptly named, a rich landscape of rolling hills and manor houses. In contrast to Dublin, the village was peaceful. From our farmhouse room all we could hear were birds twittering, a dog barking intermittently in the distance, and then utter silence. At breakfast it was Kathleen Phelan's musical voice, speaking about her five grown children, telling of the hard times that many in Prosperous had fallen upon, and offering her sympathy for our troubles: "Ah, you're on holiday. You shouldn't have to watch your bags every second. If you have to do that sort of thing you might as well stay home, lock the door, and watch *Far and Away*." Kathleen Phelan's husband had been forced into an early retirement, and she had felt compelled to open up her home as a bed-and-breakfast. She was a lovely woman—as a matter of fact, "lovely" was her favorite word—but she seemed slightly upset over this twist of fate. She never turned on the heat in our room, and I will always wonder if there was some subconscious revenge at work. Her children were grown and successful, and she loved them dearly. Her house was frayed around the edges but it was a substantial place. Her story, it seemed to me, was of the landed gentry in decline, but there was a bigger story: as a friend said to me, "Ireland is the only third world country in Europe, an economic as well as a geographical afterthought."

The population of Ireland in the 1830s was over six million, but by the early twentieth century that was cut in half. Now it is three and a half million people, the country never having fully recovered from the failure of the potato crop and emigration. Smaller than Cuba, Ireland has been a tiny, sea-bound country for nearly nine thousand years, since the time after the Ice Age when it separated from Europe along with England. Within three thousand years it was cut off from Britain, and the first settlers who came from Scandinavia to England crossed the narrow straits to Ireland. A tribal society emerged, families and clans, a rural society—one described by Anthony Burgess as "an environment agricultural, traditional, and imbrued with a sense of historical wrong." Some say that Irish history began with St. Patrick, for he was the author of the earliest documents known to have been written in the country. Monasteries became the closest thing to towns until the Vikings and Normans left their mark—seaports, roads, bridges, churches, cities. For the Irish, though, it was one conqueror after another, one absentee landlord after the next. The Irish rebelled. They are still rebelling, but the agricultural society, the sense of tribes and clans, remains strong, despite what Burgess described as "the paradox of a green land dedicated to powerful faith and rural tranquility being torn by urban struggles."

Unemployment is at 22 percent in Ireland, and the lack of opportunity may have created an exilic mentality. As one young Irishwoman said to me in a pub in Youghal, "We take pride in our education in this country. We just don't have anywhere to use it." In the same pub, another man, this one an expatriate from America, said, "Things are not always, or perhaps ever, logical in Ireland. When people complain about car accidents or littering, the government passes a law to fine litterers or lower the speed limit. Then they don't enforce the laws. That way everybody's happy. This is a country of good news and bad news. The bad news is we have the highest unemployment rate in Europe. The good news is that all the unemployed are working. A man can make 110 percent on the dole and have a side job besides."

This man described for me the Ireland depicted with black Celtic humor in Roddy Doyle's novels featuring the Rabbittes, a struggling middle-class family portrayed in books such as *The Commitments* and *The Snapper*. *The Snapper*, for instance, centers upon the twenty-year-old Sharon Rabbitte's out-of-wedlock pregnancy. The book is filled with outraged exclamations—"Jaysis" and "tha' fuckin eejit"—and absurdist comedy:

> —It says my perception might be heightened when I'm pregnant.
> —Yeh smell arigh' from here, love, said Jimmy Sr. He leaned over.
> —What's the buke abou'?
> —Pregnancy.
> —Jaysis, d'yeh need a buke to be pregnant these days?
> —I didn't have a book, said Veronica.
> —Shhh! went Jimmy Sr.
> —You woudn't've been able to read it, Ma, said Darren.
> The remote control hit his shoulder and bounced off his head.

This scene reminds me of the Ireland we encountered in a few of the pubs in the southern part of the country. In Youghal we stopped in Moby Dick's, a pub renamed by its owner Kevin "Paddy" Linehan after John Huston made his film of Melville's masterpiece in the town, using the bar as the location for Peter Coffin's Spouter Inn. There were five or six men at the bar and two young boys sitting at one of the booths when we walked in. A television was on, showing Gregory Peck, a supernatural white streak across his cheek, speaking in the Shakespearean tones of Ahab. A few men in the bar resembled Richard Basehart, who portrayed Ishmael in the movie, but not one looked like Queequeg. And no one paid any attention to the film, which seemed to be a visual Muzak in the place. Not even six-year-old Gerald or five-year-old Kevin gave it any notice. "I saw it before, about ten times," said Kevin. Gerald said, "I've seen it eleven."

Youghal was Huston's stand-in for New Bedford, Massachusetts, the whaling village from which the *Pequod* sailed in pursuit of Moby Dick. Youghal may look more like a nineteenth-century New England coastal village than most towns in Massachusetts, but it is actually a walled seaport known for the Collegiate Church of St. Mary, the oldest church in Ireland, and for Sir Walter Raleigh's brief sojourn there as Lord Mayor of the town. Of course, the feelings about Raleigh, the man who introduced the potato crop to the country, are ambivalent.

Youghal is a town of moss-covered stone walls and crumbling turrets. In the graveyard of St. Mary's, tombstones lean together in the lush grass like old friends huddling against the elements. During the day the streets are crowded with red-cheeked people intent on going from one place to another. But at night, the people seem willing to be still, to discuss future glories built perhaps on bad memories. As Lawrence Millman wrote, "A people with a feel for the delights of human talk let their doorsteps rot with green moss; they are not concerned with what they see, only with what they hear. And so they grant ruins a staunch visibility in their countryside, where the ruins are the most ruinous in Europe."

That night, as we sat at the bar of the Nook, waiting for the music to begin in the adjoining room, a well-fed little man walked in to a round of greetings. He reminded me of the character in Seamus Heaney's poem "Casualty," who

> . . . drank like a fish
> Nightly, naturally
> Swimming towards the lure
> Of warm lit-up places,
> The blurred mesh and murmur
> Drifting among glasses
> In the gregarious smoke.

The bartender said, "How's the farm, John?"

"Rotten," he replied. "I'm just here to fill a prescription . . . a pint of dark, if you don't mind." It wasn't until an hour later, when John and I were in the midst of our own conversation, that I asked him about his life as a farmer and found out that the question was "How is your *form*," or health. At that, the men laughed and gathered around me. I became a sort of curiosity, but they also wanted me to understand the Irish character better, even if I never mastered the language:

"I was in America once," one explained, "and saw a funeral. The people all acted like business as usual. No one stopped. I couldn't understand that."

"In England if you ask two questions, they call a solicitor. In Ireland if you ask two questions, they give you three answers."

"I damn the IRA to the darkest hell."

"My whole family has strayed from Catholicism. I remember when I was a boy, one of my classmates had done some miching, you know, doing the dodge from school, and the Christian Brothers caught him, tied his hands behind his back, and whipped him with a bamboo stick. That did me for Catholicism."

"I was riding on a train to Limerick years ago, sitting next to a man who never spoke a word until we were nearly there when he said one thing, 'Jaysis, I hate work.' Then he fell silent. He never spoke again for the rest of the trip, but I've always remembered that beautifully articulated philosophy that ranks with the wisdom of Aristotle."

England/Ireland

"You know why they invented liquor, don't you? Two reasons. First, so that the Irish couldn't take over the world. Second, so that every ugly woman would have a ride home at the end of the night."

"I asked my friend Murphy if he talks to his wife while he's making love, and he said, 'Certainly, if there's a phone handy.'"

The jokes and stories came in a flood of words—lyrical and poetic, crude and blunt, polite and meandering. The atmosphere in the pub didn't seem that different from the one in Darby O'Gills, a bar that was a social center in the Bronx when I grew up. The resemblance seemed even stronger when the music started up in the next room—"Wait Til' the Midnight Hour," "Jumpin' Jack Flash," "Knockin' on Heaven's Door"—like a call from the 1970s. The room was packed with young men and women, listening to their own music—and mine, it seemed—and, like their parents next door, drinking the dark Celtic brew in a smoke-filled room.

Western Ireland is another world entirely, starkly beautiful, a rocky coast of bogs and winding paths, mountains rising into low hanging mists, golden grass, long-haired sheep and curious donkeys, a Druidic landscape where night falls upon mounds of peat bricks placed like sculpted domes along the sides of roads. At night the eyes of Connemara sheep blaze green against the headlights of oncoming cars. On our way to the village of

Cleggan, which stands against a "white breast of the dim sea," we drove a mile down a narrow road to Thoor Ballylee Castle, Yeats's summer home. It was exactly as he described it, the river encircling the property, the thatched-roof house, and the ancient stone tower, which once separated him from the world. Only a stone bridge connected the property and the countryside around it. The shadow of a bird brushed the corner of the tower and I imagined Yeats for a moment pacing the battlements, looking on the world:

> Tree, like a sooty finger, start from the earth;
> And send imagination forth. . . .

This place became his Lake Isle of Innisfree, the water lapping, the evening full of linnets' wings, the crickets' song, a place where peace came dropping slow into the deep heart's core. A few miles away was Coole Park, Lady Gregory's estate where Yeats spent much of his time. Next to the ruins of Coole Mansion are magnificent gardens surrounded by a ten-foot-high stone wall, silent woods, a pond. Lady Gregory's was a haven for artists. A copper beech tree in the center of the garden has Sean O'Casey's, George Bernard Shaw's, and Yeats's initials carved into it, a reminder of who roamed the wooded paths. It is a dreamy sort of environment, as unlike Joyce's Dublin as one could imagine, a perfect stillness, where Yeats could enter Byzantium, and sing of "what is past, or passing, or to come."

England/Ireland

*Bravery's a treasure in a lonesome place, and a
lad would kill his father, I'm thinking, would
face a foxy divil with a pitchpike on the flags
of hell.*

> —John Millington Synge,
> *Playboy of the Western World*

That night in Cleggan a keening wind moaned along the coast. It seemed to be a country for old men, their faces chiseled like Connemara marble. In a pub in nearby Clifden a fiddle player, his fingers like tongues of flame, seemed like one of Yeats's figures cut from lapis lazuli, his eyes glittering and gay. As he played, to the far west a stronger wind screamed along the eastern coast of the United States, producing the "storm of the century," but to the northeast the wind barely whispered through Drumcliff Churchyard where, under bare Ben Bulben's head, Yeats's words were cut into a limestone marker:

> Cast a cold eye
> On life, on death.
> Horseman, pass by!

Like an ancient rune, those words led me home. As we drove through Galway City I saw a group of children playing basketball in a schoolyard. The rims were bent, and the girls and boys appeared to be inexpert at the game. They reminded me that my sons were probably playing the same game at that very moment thousands of miles away if the storm had subsided. Thinking of them, I recalled a twenty-year-old woman named Rosemary whom I had met in a pub in Youghal. At the end of the night, when the musicians had left the stage, she took up her guitar at our table and sang. She never said why she chose Cat Stevens's "Father and Son," but I felt she sang it for me. Her voice was sweet and soft. The words about youth and change, a father's practical advice—"For you will still be here tomorrow / But your dreams may not"—sounded familiar. So did the son's response—that the father's advice was "the same, same old story" and that the only answer for the son was to leave. Those words sounded familiar. Had I heard them as a young man? Had I spoken them to my sons? I hoped not. As she sang the son's response her voice rose, vibrated as if these words were truly hers: "How can I try to explain / When I do he turns away again . . ." I wondered if I had seen those words written in the face of my oldest son. I thought of myself as a boy, listening for stories. Then, heading home, I imagined I heard the shouts of my sons and my own voice telling them that, like Christy Mahon in *Playboy of the Western World*, if they had courage their dreams would place them "on the springtide of the stars of luck."

PART THREE

THE FUTURE

The child is father of the man.
                    —William Wordsworth,
                      "My Heart Leaps Up"

CHAPTER 7

THE PLAYGROUND

*The ball loved Flick. . . . His hands were like
wild birds.*

> —John Updike,
> "Ex-Basketball Player"

The most purely American game. . . .

> —George F. Will,
> "Basketball's Birthday"

Only connect . . .

> —E. M. Forster, *Howard's End*

When it left my hand I knew it was going in. It rolled
lazily, the seams spinning backwards as if the ball were
floating on water, not air. I blew on my hands, which
were red and chafed from the cold, and watched the ball
arc and then drop with a sudden metallic click through
the chainlink net.

I was about twelve years old, standing alone in the

playground behind St. Philip Neri Elementary School, snow shoveled to the sides of the court, my breath sputtering out in short smoky bursts as I whispered to myself, "Haahhr. The crowd roars. Pearson scores the winning basket!"

For me the playground was a separate world. In a way it was connected to my love of books. As with reading, when I was playing basketball, time stopped. The world disappeared and at the same instant came into clearer focus. When I was alone on the playground, I felt a luxuriant loneliness, the way you can feel on a gray, brittle day in February when your own hand seems to be the most visible object in the whole world. I watched myself perform, wishing I were one of Pete Axthelm's young men "who flashed briefly across the asphalt courts, momentarily suspended in time and memory." Alone, I was lifted into the purely physical, leaping in the cold air to take a jump shot, dribbling full court, the ball thumping against the ground in sync with my heart. I spent hours driving for layups and maneuvering for off-balance hook shots. I imagined opponents, dreamed of spectacular feats, and transformed thought into action.

But most of the time there was a crowd in the playground. At those moments of intense competition the court contracted to a small universe, and as sportswriter Jeff Greenfield has said, the game became a "struggle for the edge," with half steps and half seconds and slight head fakes meaning everything. The smallest maneuver might determine victory when the margins were so tight. In this narrow world I could see the chaotic larger world reflected in a shape I understood. It was all there, played out in small dramas—selfishness, anger, apathy, courage, foolishness, devotion . . . I saw myself and my friends pretty clearly at times on that ninety-four-foot by fifty-foot stage.

Perhaps what I liked most about our games, though, was that they were different from ordinary experience. As Rick Telander wrote a few years ago, "Games are not like life, no matter what your eighth-grade coach told you. They are wonderfully *unlike* life in that they have specific beginnings and ends, precise rules, pre-scribed boundaries, judges, penalties, timeouts and, at the end, losers and winners." Also, it seemed to me that simple Protestant values—perseverance, team work, hard-earned skill—all added up to success. Of course, there was always some luck, a secular version of Calvin-ist grace, but generally basketball offered some certainty and order. The best won.

Bill Bradley said that it was the swish, the sound of the dribble, the feel of going up in the air that attracted him to the game. Pete Axthelm, partly echoing Frost's comment about poetry providing a "momentary stay against confusion," called the game a "brief and neces-sary escape from reality." But for me it felt less like an escape than like Frost's momentary stay. The game had high drama, sharp conflict, and strong characters, and even if it didn't have the profound feeling of poetry, it did—momentarily at least—place order on the world. And always connected to it was the pure thrill of physicality. The feel of the scarred rubber ball; the cracks in the uneven courts; the chipped paint flapping on the pole; the smell of sweat; the perfect pitch of the ball snapping in the net; the pleasant, aching bone-tiredness after hours of play.

> *I remember we used to practice in the gym in high school; then, on the way home, we'd stop and play on the playgrounds until eight o'clock. I played when I was cold and my body was aching and I was so tired . . . and don't know why, I just kept playing and playing.*
> —Larry Bird, *On Basketball*

The sound of the basketball pounding against the driveway is rhythmic. For the past half hour Ian, who is fourteen, has been dribbling behind his back, between his legs, flipping the ball up at the basket right-handed and left-handed. In a few minutes Owen, who is ten, appears. Their eighteen-year-old brother Shane stops for a few minutes on his way to his girlfriend's house, just enough time to play a game of twenty-one. When he leaves, two other boys show up. A game begins.

Their court is even more narrow than mine was over twenty-five years ago. The driveway they play on every day after school is eighteen feet wide. The length of the portion of the driveway they use is only about twice as long. Their game is modern, media influenced, full of talk. As a boy, my game was silent until an argument erupted over a foul—denials, sneers, threats about quitting, finally someone's grudging capitulation. These boys have the same fights and disagreements, and as many of them as we used to have. The difference is that they fill what for my friends and me would have been aggressive silences with constant talk, an in-your-face, prime-time, MTV repartee that is like rap lyrics to match the beat of the ball:

"C'mon Jim, you can't stop that shot. You might as well sit down, boy. All you can do is watch."

"All I *have* to do is watch. With bricks like you throw up, you could build a new house."

"Get off me . . . go home. I'm unstoppable, baby. You can't check me, scrub. . . ."

All this said in the frenetic, high-volumed intonation of sportscaster Dick Vitale. It doesn't seem as if anyone ever wins the game or the war of words, for nearly every afternoon the contest is renewed but the score is rarely announced. The boys drift along on the strip of cement as if it were a river of dreams.

Often, I play basketball too, sometimes with my friends but mostly with my sons. Shane can jump higher than I ever could. Ian can dribble like Pistol Pete and makes me feel clumsy just watching him. Owen seems too good to be only ten, with a court vision that might make Bill Bradley jealous. Our games, particularly between Shane and me, used to have some of the resonances of the conflict depicted in *The Great Santini* but have become mellow and playful in recent years.

Now, as we play, their dreams and my memories flow together, as if past and future streamed into some immanent present. With each bounce of the basketball the seconds tick toward a yielding future reflected in their eyes—thirty-foot jump shots at the buzzer to win a high school championship game, a no-look pass bounced between a defender's legs to win the NCAA finals, or two perfect foul shots against the Los Angeles Lakers in the playoffs. Their clear blue eyes are fixed intently on distances. Mine look inward, toward a less yielding past. And somewhere in between, the four of us know, is the truth, at some point where dreams and memories merge into what the world will allow.

But, perhaps, in games this is the simple truth: dreams are necessary.

> *For now he knew what Shalimar knew: If you*
> *surrender to the air, you could ride it.*
> —Toni Morrison, *Song of Solomon*

John Kelly sits across the table from me, his handsome, ruddy face shadowed by stubble and his graying hair mostly hidden by a red baseball cap with "Guadalcanal

1st Marines" stitched into it. His steely blue eyes glint with enthusiasm behind brown-rimmed glasses as he talks about basketball.

When he discovered the game as a sixth-grader at Braddock Road Boys' Club in Springfield, Virginia, he fell in love with a sport that seemed to allow him to soar out of the world, to escape into his own body. That year he won the championship for twelve-year-olds, and the successes continued regularly from that moment on. In eighth grade he made the high school freshman team, in ninth the J. V., and in the tenth grade he was the point guard for the varsity. As he got closer to his slim six-foot-two-inch full height, he became a shooting guard and small forward. By 1975 he was playing for Rutgers under coach Tom Young. He spent four years there, improving his defense, becoming a better scorer, and dreaming about the NBA.

In 1978, Rutgers played against Indiana State University and Larry Bird. They beat Bird's team by one point, he tells me, as he winks at the young waitress who has come up to take our order at Kelly's Pub in Norfolk. (Even though he's not related to the owner of the restaurant, he seems to be familiar with all the waitresses.) He flirts, our waitress smiles shyly, and when she walks away he gives me an innocent look that seems to say, "Yeah, I was an altar boy a long time ago, but now I play basketball on Sundays instead of going to Mass."

The thirty-six-year-old Kelly moved around quite a bit growing up. His father was a career officer in the marines, and that accounts for his birth in Oceanside, California, his first three years in Japan, and stops in North Carolina, New York, and Virginia along the way. It accounts for many of his deepest influences as well.

His father spent thirty-four years in the service and fought in three wars, spending time in the South Pacific, in Korea, and finally taking a tour in Vietnam so that the Marine Corps would allow him to complete his college degree. In 1982, three years after his son had finished his degree at Rutgers, he was a fifty-eight-year-old senior at Syracuse University. Nine years later he died, struck to the ground near the 18th green by a heart attack, as the secretary of the air force looked on in disbelief.

His father was a drill instructor for many years, as tough as any image portrayed on the screen by John Wayne, but John Kelly remembers a man of sensibility and rectitude, not a cold-eyed bully. From his father he learned respect for ideas, how to act with honor and dignity, how to treat people with understanding. But although John's father was a gentle man, he was also a marine officer, and when John or his older brother got too far out of line, they felt his belt come down with stinging force across their outstretched palms. "You couldn't wipe your ass or put on your socks for a few days with that hand," John recalls. "Whatever the lesson was, you learned it fast and you remembered it."

But his father taught him much more lasting lessons. Not many marine majors brought their sons down to

Washington, D.C., to see the peace marches. Marine or not, his father was open to the world of ideas and listened to other points of view. He even seemed ready to accept some of his younger son's searching for a path in the world. After college John spent his summers as a lifeguard and as a player in the Jersey Shore Pro League, competing against the likes of Kelly Tripuka, Gus Williams, Charles Barkley, and Mark Eaton, whom he remembers as a giant whose head alone seemed to be as big as the backboard.

Thousands of great players, on the brink of the professional level, play in such leagues—the Baker League in Philadelphia, Rucker in New York City, or the Jersey Shore—essentially a collection of minor leagues, just below European play and the CBA in terms of entrance into the NBA. John played for a team sponsored by Phoenix Business Systems with Rory Sparrow, who has had a long, productive career in the NBA, at the other guard; the six-foot-eleven-inch Tom Broderick at center; and the six-foot-nine-inch John Ebeling at power forward, a young man who was a first division player in Italy, a "human highlight film who dunked on everybody."

John was paid fifty dollars per game to play on outdoor courts with perforated metal backboards and often unimaginable wind currents. Players would have to take into account the breeze and keep a careful eye out for the backboard supports. It reminded John of his earlier days playing on the Luzon Street Courts behind Walter

The Playground

Reed Hospital in Washington, D.C., and getting paid for it each night as well. Besides, it was like having a free ticket to great street theater. He learned a lot watching the games. The day before he was to play against the current Orlando Magic star Scott Skiles, he went to see his team play.

Skiles, a young man who had experienced some problems with drugs and alcohol, was just going through the motions on the court. He had made his name, won bigger battles, and seemed interested only in a leisurely game. He was playing against a fourth-round draft choice for the Knicks, a young man looking to make his mark. The young man hand-checked Skiles, then he grabbed his shirt, his shorts, and finally he started reciting the poetry of the court. "You ain't all that much! Who said you could play ball?"

It went beyond the euphoria of the game's bubbling up into the verbal, where words soar into an arrogant sort of poetry, Beowulf's challenge to the monster. In this situation words fly upward or they flutter to the ground, and the talker may have to scoop them up, eat crow. At a certain point Skiles said, "You better quit, or I'm going to go for fifty against you tonight." His opponent just hand-checked harder and talked louder.

"That's it," said Skiles, "I'm going for fifty against your fat ass." Saying it, he slapped the young man's hand away from his shirt and drove past him for a layup. On defense he stole the ball and threw a no-look pass for another easy basket. He never relented on either end of the court. He scored fifty-one points. The young man never made it into the pros. The next day when he matched up against Skiles, John never opened his mouth. John's team lost but Skiles didn't score close to fifty points.

It was around this time that John's father said to him, 'You've screwed around long enough with basketball. Go to graduate school." John spent the next two years at William and Mary, working on his M.A. and writing a thesis on the fiction of William Faulkner, and in 1981 he received his degree. When he speaks about Faulkner's work his eyes light with the same fire they do when he speaks of basketball. His face scrunches up into a jumble of angles as he recalls an image or a line of prose. His demonstrative hands, long, thin fingers pirouetting like white-knuckled figures in the air, dance in the background to his words.

But in 1981 basketball still held him more than Faulkner, perhaps, because he left for Southern Ireland to play in the British Isles Professional League. The four years he spent playing in Ireland were like being in the NBA in the early 1950s, barnstorming from one town to another. If the crowd didn't like a team, they would spit on their heads as they entered the gymnasium. It wasn't uncommon to see the crowd throw all sorts of objects, anything from ice cubes to something more substantial like scorching coins heated on the lights. The conditions were often so primitive that the more modern facilities would have a sign outside the gym that said, "Games will be heated," which didn't allude to the competitive fire of the teams but to the temperature of the arena.

Basketball had made some inroads but Ireland was then still a country of blood sports, like coursing, and traditional European athletics, like football. Pete Strickland, another American basketball player in Ireland at the time, sums up the experience with a story. Strickland and another American pro were asked to go to a women's high school to do a coaching session for about two hours. They went to the school and met the headmistress, who told them how much the girls looked forward to the training session. After they talked for a while, Strickland asked where the gym was.

"Gym?" she replied. "Oh, we don't have one of those, but you're welcome to work with the girls in the cafeteria."

Strickland and his partner exchanged quick, desperate glances, wondering what they would teach seventy-five young girls about basketball without any baskets. After a whispered conference, they decided on passing and dribbling techniques.

"Could you show us where the basketballs are kept?" Strickland asked.

"Oh, we don't have any of those," the headmistress said, leaving them in the cafeteria to wait for their trainees.

Strickland and his partner spent two hours working on defense, shadowing drills and the like. The next time he came with his own basketballs, but he thought that the young women seemed disappointed to have these foreign objects intrude on their game of defense.

Such stories were true for John Kelly as well. In Southern Ireland he found the same "neanderthal conditions" that Strickland had. It was in Northern Ireland that he found the most modern facilities, subsidized by the British in the hopes that such places would help keep kids off the streets and Molotov cocktails out of their hands. During John's first season in Ireland his team, North Mon, traveled to Northern Ireland for a game against Sporting Belfast. As they drove down Falls Road, which snakes like a line in the sand dividing the Catholic and Protestant sections of the city, John watched teenaged British soldiers, patrolling with ever-watchful eyes and M-16's pointed, as if they were in enemy territory during a war. John's team drove through the kind of area where informants were "knee-capped" and car bombings seemed to be common occurrences. That Saturday morning a wall painter riding to work had stopped at a traffic light, and his car back-fired twice. Before the second backfire was much more than an aftersound, a British patrol had put over one hundred rounds into the car and driver.

In their van, the team passed British outposts in the middle of the city. They also drove past a housing project where a child of about eight or nine years old was standing in the shadows. Since John was the only player looking out the van's windows, he was the only one to see the boy step out of the gutted doorway and fire a rock at the back of the bus, striking it like a gun report. All the passengers in the bus but John hit the floor, and the driver raced off.

North Mon's game against Sporting Belfast had the same violent atmosphere, angry crowds and sharp elbows. Some of the younger players for North Mon found it difficult to concentrate with a bearded Belfast fan who sat directly across from their bench, pointing his index finger like the barrel of a gun, cocking his thumb, and squinting with a sinister smile throughout the game. North Mon lost by over thirty points.

The second time they played Sporting Belfast John scored forty points himself, and the game was supposed to go into overtime. A Belfast guard hit a jump shot from the far corner in the last second as John leaped with both hands up and felt the rush of air as the ball sailed just over his reaching fingertips. But this was the first time that an electronic scoreboard was used in Parochial Hall, and there was a discrepancy with the scoresheet, which John said looked like an annotated version of "The Waste Land." Somehow, when the numbers were all added up, Sporting Belfast won 97–96, and the bearded fan walked out of the hall with his hands in his pockets.

In 1985, John's last year in Ireland, his team won the National Cup but, as he says, "In the European contest we ran into the Yugoslav team and they whipped our ass." Around this time his father began to speak again of "gainful employment," and John returned to the states, first to teach and coach in a Williamsburg high school and then to work as an assistant basketball coach under Tom Young at Old Dominion University.

When a coup forced Young out, all the assistant coaches went too. This left John as a part-time college teacher and a tennis instructor. Basketball remained serious play for him, like writing poetry. At one time basketball had been his universe, even if his tryout with the New Jersey Nets in 1979 had not led to the NBA. Nevertheless, basketball had always given him a sense of place. He remembers Dave Bing talking about his last years in the pros. He was nearly blind in one eye. Before he shot the ball he would look down at the court and sight his feet. He would see where he was on the floor and release the ball accordingly, blind but somehow knowing exactly where he was. Without his glasses, John is nearly legally blind but on the court he can always see where he is.

John talks about basketball in aesthetic terms, the rhythms of the ball, the quality of a move, the structure of a pick and roll. "Everybody's shooting for those moments of beauty," he says. "The game lifts us out of our daily concerns into a pattern so physical we rise above ourselves. The game becomes a rehearsal for living— offering lessons about generosity and pride and luck and courage and acceptance."

Toward the end of our lunch at Kelly's we talk about one of the NBA playoff games in which former ODU star Chris Gatling watched helplessly as Shawn Kemp flew past him and dunked the ball with such force that it rocketed through the net and bounced off his head. "You have to put a cape on that fucker," John says speaking of Kemp, "and add the *S*." But as we leave the restaurant and John returns the red cap to his head, it is poetry and Faulkner and his father that we talk about. John remembers his father teaching him what the game has taught him, what Faulkner taught him—"the old verities and truths of the heart . . . love and honor and pity and pride and compassion and sacrifice." For the second time John tells me about two of his poems that were recently accepted for publication. The time he scored fifty-one points in a game in Ireland he barely mentioned once in our conversations. His father he has spoken of often.

> *He became his father.*
> —Walker Percy, *The Second Coming*

It was about seventy degrees, a steel gray day, the breeze from the ocean just sharp enough to cut through the spaces between the towering hotels on the Virginia Beach strip. Atlantic Avenue, usually clogged with cars and tourists, was swarming with basketball players, and the side streets were dotted with portable hoops.

The "Hoops It Up" tournament had come to Virginia Beach, and as far as I could tell we were the only father-son team among a field of a few hundred entries. Shane,

Ian, and I were to play, and Owen was to be our coach. This meant our ages ranged from fourteen to forty-two, our heights from five feet to slightly under six feet, and our coach was ten. But the sun was beginning to melt the clouds, and we were the Asphalt All Stars, ready for anything.

During the warmups for our first game, one of our opponents, a slim, muscular twenty-year-old, stood under the basket, sprung effortlessly into the air and dunked the ball backwards. He repeated his performance—just in case we hadn't noticed, perhaps. We had.

Ian didn't feel quite ready for this game; therefore, our fourth man on the roster, Palmer Rutherford, an athletic thirty-year-old, stood in for him. We lost anyway but only by 16 to 14. Each basket counted for one point, and any shot beyond twenty feet counted for two. For me it was one of those playground games when I knew each time the ball left my hands it was going in the basket. But, finally, we weren't able to deal with a twenty-year-old leaper.

Our next game was a few hours later against a team called Pure Domination. None of us was looking forward to this game. Pure Domination was described in the tournament magazine as a group of twenty-year-olds, one of whom had played high school varsity basketball. Ian, in particular, looked depressed.

Seconds before the game began, I talked Ian into playing. What did we have to lose? At first he was a bit tentative, but soon he was dribbling through his legs, behind his back, shooting high, floating rainbow layups over the outstretched hands of defenders. Quickly he had four in a row. After about twenty minutes the score was tied, 14–14. Each team had a chance to go ahead, but both tried for a win, letting the ball fly from behind the two-point line. We were just lucky first. Shane grabbed a rebound, I backpedaled to the right side of the two-point semicircle, and he rifled a pass. Off balance, I let the ball go as a defender's hand fluttered past my face. And although the spin felt wrong and I knew the ball wasn't going in, it did. We won and it felt a bit like winning a place in the Final Four. We high-fived and laughed and dreamed of working our way toward the championship.

But by our next game, against Steel Service, our legs (at least mine) had given out. The index finger on my left hand was taped by the ambulance driver on duty. He was pretty sure it was broken. Shane and Ian both played well in that final game. Owen cheered us on and called a timeout or two, but we lost 16 to 12. We felt like winners, though. Each game had been close, we had won one game, and we had played together as a team.

As we drove home, talking about particular plays, blown chances, and lucky shots, it wasn't basketball that was on my mind. It was fathers and sons. My own father had played baseball with me once, hitting fungoes out to Patty Dougherty and me at Harris Field in the Bronx when I was in grammar school. We had never played with or competed against one another. But nearly half of my life had been spent playing with my sons—volleying on the tennis courts, tossing a football, catching a baseball, and most often, shooting baskets, having games of twenty-one and horse and when they got old enough two on two.

Some of our games had produced angry words, but nothing stopped us from playing together. In play we had always been a part of one another, had always sensed how our blood flowed together. Nick Lyons once wrote, "The search for a father is a search for authority outside of yourself; you feel wraithlike, incomplete without him, in whatever form he takes. Too much 'father,' as Kafka knew, makes the will go mush—too little and the longing can be monstrous." I knew that I had had both too much and too little, and I wondered how my own sons would feel in a decade or so. Would they recall our contests with the same pleasure that I did? Would they miss them when age or distance made them impossible to recapture? Would I seem to them to be too much of a father because the other possibility seemed unlikely? Would they regret that they hadn't had the same freedom that photographer Richard Benson described in not having had a father?

I had spent half of my life trying to be the father that I wished I had had. The search for father that pervades American literature, from *Huckleberry Finn* to *All the King's Men*, had seeped into my soul. But the father I had searched for was inside of me. I tried to create him and in the process, perhaps, had doomed myself to regrets over many little failures. Certainly sons are their fathers, but fathers, too, are their sons. That is why we feel their pain, their anger, their mistakes. That is why we are horrified by their weaknesses. They're ours. But that is also why we feel such tenderness and love.

Between fathers and sons, silences can sometimes mean great things. Our communications are often laconic, mysterious. Anger, longing, fear, and joy become twisted strands in a knotted bundle of meaning. At times we communicate through action. We find our words in movement—floating downriver on a raft or reaching for a pass on the basketball court. Like Huck, maybe we sometimes find our fathers in those neutral zones, the rivers or the courts, where civilization is held at bay, where we are able to forget the world for a few hours and in the silence listen to our own hearts and feel our bodies move together in harmony.

> *Between the wish and the thing the world lies waiting.*
>
> —Cormac McCarthy,
> *All the Pretty Horses*

It's their eyes I notice first, wide and blue as the sky. Their faces are flushed, and their blond hair matted darkly against foreheads. On different ends of the Old Dominion University gym two of my sons, Owen and

Ian, dribble the ball, move around screens and shoot. My eyes, rushing back and forth between the two games, sense the shots coming but miss each in the desperate attempt to see them both simultaneously. But both go in. I can tell from the snapping angle of the nets and a double smile, suppressed but surfacing in their eyes and lifting the corners of my mouth.

When the games are over, the players gather in the bleachers on this last day of summer camp. The parents sit behind them. Eventually the thin, coltish legs stretch out, the sounds of dozens of basketballs striking against the hardwood court fade, and the faintly sour smell of heat and sweat settles on the floor like dew. The boys sit there, exhausted and happy, like the spectators in William Carlos Williams's poem "At the Ball Game": "a spirit of uselessness / delights them / all the exciting detail of the chase / and the escape / the flash of genius— / all to no end save beauty / the eternal—"

Of course, some sense of order and beauty is not always the driving force in sports. As Jim Naughton wrote in a recent book about Michael Jordan: ". . . sports, for better and worse, functions as a long-running public morality play. In an increasingly fragmented society, sports provides a common language in which to speak of good and evil, promise and disappointment, authenticity and fraudulence, justice and revenge." Probably the most romantic notions about sports, like the idea of the marines shaping a youngster's moral vision, are simply foolishness. Rather, as the sometimes dour basketball coach John Wooden put it, "Sports don't build character; they reveal it."

As the coaches bring in boxes of camp shirts and basketballs and line the tables with trophies for the winning teams, my thoughts drift back to a three-on-three tournament that I recently played in at Old Dominion. Two of my colleagues in the English Department, Jeb Midgett and John Kelly, were my teammates. My son Ian was our substitute. The competition was internal, college varsity players who had finished their careers last year or the year before or very good playground players. I was a bit out of my depth, but John Kelly, luckily, took the ball to the basket whenever it was necessary. Ian got to play, and he played well. And we won the championship. Before we did, however, some character was revealed.

During our next-to-the-last game, which was fiercely and loudly contested, amidst our grunts and arguments, I heard a loud slap. But our world had contracted to the half court we were on and none of us paid any attention. When our game was done—we won, although the score was disputed by our opponents—I noticed a campus police officer, wearing surgical gloves, poking under the mats and examining the perimeter of the gym.

"What are you looking for?" I asked.

Without raising his eyes, he said, "A finger."

"A what?"

"A finger. An index finger."

Then I noticed the blood splattered all over the walls and the floor. One of the trainers walked in with a bag filled with a pink liquid, what I quickly realized was melted ice and blood. He too looked for the finger. But it was never found. And although I could not imagine where the top three-quarters of an inch of index finger could have gone, as if it were some sentient piece of flesh in a story by Edgar Allan Poe, I wondered more about why a young man would get that upset over a missed shot, so angry that he would smash his hand against the wall, ramming it against the ladder bolted there, and severing the top half of his finger.

It's the voice of Pete Strickland, one of the assistant coaches at the camp, that brings me back to the present. Ian walks up shyly to receive an award as one of the campers of the day. A few minutes later Strickland talks enthusiastically about the young man who has been awarded the camper of the week trophy: "He is the kind of player that every coach wants to have," Strickland says. "This is a young man who sat with perfect attention when our guest speakers gave pointers. This is a player who played 100 percent every game but played with sportsmanship. I'm happy to give this award to Owen Pearson." A surge of emotion catches me off guard. I'm proud of my sons—not for their skill but for their tenacity, their hopefulness, their ambition. I know that the emotion I feel is pride, but it is mixed with sadness, a knowledge of how often their struggles will end in some sort of failure, how many rejections await them, how tough the world can be on anyone's dreams.

But as I see my son's face, a smile held carefully in check as the boys' code seems to demand, I notice his eyes, cheerful and knowing. Then I look at the world, at the future, through those eyes, and I see a world laced with light and mystery. Through his eyes I see the world, and I have at that moment few doubts about the odds. They are, it seems without question, in his favor, the future laid out before him like a field of opportunity and accident, love and sadness: life for him to live.

Epilogue

*. . . the feeling that comes when you first notice
your life turning into a story.*

—Norman Maclean,
"USFS 1919: The Ranger,
the Cook, and a Hole in the Sky"

Right before I left Berkeley, California, after finishing
graduate school, I had one last game of basketball at
Live Oak Park and said goodbye to a few friends. One
of them gave me a parting gift: a used Signet paperback
copy of Walker Percy's *The Last Gentleman*. The book
had no cover, was stamped LIBRARY DISCARD, marked
five cents, and had an amoeba-shaped water stain covering its title page.

It was 1972 and probably seemed the perfect gift for
one existentialist basketball player with a ponytail to
give another as he embarked on a three-thousand-mile
journey back to the East Coast. It was the right gift. I
still have the book. It has survived a fire in Vermont and

a flood in Virginia. I have read it too many times to count over the past twenty years.

But I didn't read it right away. It lay in a box for about a year until one day I came across it again as I rummaged through stuff to be thrown out. I'm not sure what I was searching for, but I found *The Last Gentleman*, and like *Youngblood Hawke*, Percy's much more profound novel came to me at the moment I needed to find it. I was teaching remedial reading at John F. Kennedy High School in New York City. Amidst the uniformed guards, the anger, and the inertia I began to doubt my own identity. Asking my students, whose lives seemed harsh and raw, to find the main idea in a paragraph seemed, as Sutter Vaught said in *The Last Gentleman*, "like asking a man hanging from a cliff to conjugate an irregular verb."

As I sat in the teachers' lounge during my breaks, I read *The Last Gentleman* and realized that my confusion, my sense of being cut adrift, was embodied in Will Barrett. His alienation made me see my own, his search allowed me to begin mine. Between Will Barrett and Jamie Vaught in the novel there was a communication, a making common: "Yes, and that was the wonder of it, that what was private and unspeakable before is speakable now because you speak it."

The Last Gentleman gave me a name for my experience when I was twenty-four years old and feeling as if I had gotten lost. Will Barrett was not a model but a comrade, and his story helped me to discover my own story. It was Percy's voice, sad and ironic but wise and compassionate, a voice like a father's, that told me what the world can be. It was a voice that asked me who I was, what was important to me, what path was necessary to take. It was a voice that contained deep silences, an ability to listen—a voice that permitted me to answer some of my own questions.

It is now a winter night, just after dusk. The air is brittle and sharp as cold steel against our cheeks as my youngest son, Owen, and I walk home from playing tennis. In a grey sea of clouds a three-quarter moon flickers like the beam of a lighthouse. We talk about how good the crisp air feels, about how he loves to run against the wind, and about a new book he is reading for school. I know that twenty-five years from now he'll remember this time or one like it, walking with his father through the night, how clean the cold air felt and how strong was the smell of wood smoke mixed with camellias. For a moment, walking next to him I feel as if I have exchanged bodies, that I am the son, willing my own memory of the future, watching myself live the past.

Owen reaches up to hold my hand, and I know that, finally, this is the only place that's known or worth knowing, for that matter, in the play of his imagination and mine against the world. It is here that we find the point where our soaring dreams and the hardscrabble world converge, where each can be transformed by the other.

Epilogue

And, when we sit on the living room couch together tonight, reading our books for school, stories from history and science and literature, we will remember this moment, our story, and make it part of all the stories that make us who we are. Twenty-five years from now he will have his own books to remember, his *Youngblood Hawke* and later his own *The Last Gentleman*, but I hope he will have read them to be like his father, not to find one. In stories he'll find the lessons he needs to hear, the moments of escape, the difficult truths. With any luck, books will lead him out into the world as well as more deeply into himself. And one day, perhaps, he will remember reading a book and connect it to a voice that spoke to him, filled with tenderness and love, and know it was his father's.

Acknowledgments

I am grateful to the College of Arts and Letters of Old Dominion University for grants which assisted me in the writing of this book. I would also like to thank John McPhee, Tony Hillerman, Wally Whitegoat, John Kelly, and the many people who took the time to speak with me about their lives and interests.

Library of Congress Cataloging-in-Publication Data

Pearson, Michael, 1949–
    A place that's known : essays / Michael Pearson.
        p.   cm.
    ISBN 0-87805-672-6 (alk. paper)
    1. Pearson, Michael, 1949–   . 2. English
teachers—United States—Biography.
3. Journalists—United States—Biography.
4. Books and reading—United States. I. Title.
PE64.P4A3   1994
814'.54—dc20   93-43204
                                                        CIP

British Library Cataloging-in-Publication data
available